One Rant One Rant One Rant One

Beyond the Pale

Exercises in Provocation

by Renzo Llorente

Introduction by Allan Cameron

Vagabond Voices
Sulaisiadar 'san Rudha

Vagabond Voices Publishing Ltd.
3 Sulaisiadar
An Rubha
Eilean Leòdhais / Isle of Lewis
Alba / Scotland HS2 0PU

ISBN 978-0-9560560-8-5

Printed and bound by Thomson Litho, East Kilbride

The publisher acknowledges subsidy towards this publication from Creative Scotland

For further information on Vagabond Voices, see the website, www.vagabondvoices.co.uk

For Verónica

No one has been so convinced as I of the futility of everything; and no one has taken so tragically so many futile things.

E. M. Cioran

At this stage, the question is no longer: how can the individual satisfy his own needs without hurting others, but rather: how can he satisfy his needs without hurting himself, without reproducing, through his aspirations and satisfactions, his dependence on an exploitative apparatus which, in satisfying his needs, perpetuates his servitude?

Herbert Marcuse

Aphorisms and Fragments
An introduction by Allan Cameron

This book opens Vagabond Voices' series of "Rants", which was primarily intended as a stimulus to debate on any social, political or cultural issue – yet one more attempt to resurrect that pamphleteering tradition that died out after the war and in any case had long ago left behind its golden days. According to Chambers Dictionary, a rant is "an empty declamation" (which we will avoid), "bombast", "a tirade" (most certainly) and in Scots "a noisy frolic" (which perhaps suggests the mixture of passion and wit that you will find in this book).

That no rants were forthcoming probably means that it was never a problem of demand but rather of supply. Then, a little over a year ago, we received a collection of aphorisms – "exercises in provocation" the author called them, but then all good literature is to some extent precisely that, in the sense that it challenges the reader to look at things anew. *To some extent*, and here the extent of this author's concentrated and well-aimed fire will provoke many thoughts in the reader. It is true that his native United States are the main target, and that is how it should be: satire, like charity, should always start at home, and a citizen can do his nation no greater service, or indeed compliment, than challenge its dangerous myths and areas of smug self-delusion, which of course can be found anywhere.

The extraordinary quality of the work was immediately apparent, and we do not have to agree with every aphorism to realise this – he would be failing in his primary purpose if we did. So we are delighted to open this new series with a slightly neglected genre and something quite unexpected. And much could be said about the genre, which here combines effervescence, elliptical drollness and considerable intellectual weight. Renzo Llorente refers to his creations as "fragments" rather than "aphorisms", and in this he is consciously identifying himself with a tradition that goes back to the nineteenth century in general and Nietzsche in particular. Not only had the ground been yielding up statues that were missing limbs, but more relevantly ancient texts were being discovered in highly degraded forms. This stunted art and literature appeared almost enhanced by being deprived of part of what their original artists and writers had intended. As Nietzsche himself said of one of his own works, the most important things have been left unsaid.

There is, of course, an enormous difference between the ancient fragment and the modern, more contrived one. The former is the product of vicissitudes over a period of often more than two millennia – vicissitudes that mainly had to do with physical decay imposed by passing time and a few human contributions which were equally uninterested in artistic integrity, typically wilful neglect or the hand of some censorious monk – whereas the latter where born in their fragmented state. In their case, what is excluded is excluded intentionally, and the result is in that sense complete.

Of course, the aphorism is an ancient literary form; it is less sententious than its near relation, the maxim, and if anonymous, both of these become proverbs – that great oral storehouse of popular wisdom. It could be argued that the modern fragment in no way differs from the aphoristic tradition. Writers of aphorisms or fragments eschew the idea of systems, and prefer to snipe at those who do. Their power lies in their small ambitions, and their intention is to wage a guerrilla war against the massed ranks of powerful but unmanageable ideological armies. They can only win by wearing the enemy down over a long period, but their actions are crucial.

Llorente has invented an interesting style for his fragments, which as a genre require economy of language and elegance of form. It has been commented that his left-wing politics clash with the elevated, sometimes even archaic, tone, but this should not surprise: the left, always more interested in production than consumption, has now become the principal guardian of a nineteenth-century humanistic tradition that believes in the importance of creative work in itself and takes pride in crafting and technique, whatever the cost in time and application. This ethos perhaps originated in the middle-classes, but for the left today, the freedom provided by education and creativity must be for all, whereas our consumer middle-class use a false demotic language and perceive education as a right that can be almost effortlessly attained by wealth.

Llorente has structured his work in two parts, the first for comment on individual and social behaviour and on religion, and the second on more overtly political issues. The nature of the arguments appears to have affected the style of the aphorisms: most notably they are much longer in the second part.

Beyond the Pale. Outwith the palisade. The title says more about the nature of this book than is immediately apparent. This expression for something outside the generally accepted morality or norm is of course of colonial origin, with particular reference to Ireland, where the Pale ceased to be a mere trading post or fort and became the entire area under direct English control. Beyond there were the "wyld Irysh" whose views and beliefs were considered barbaric and uncivilised. A sixteenth-century papal nuncio who travelled extensively in the area beyond the Pale had enough self-awareness to state, "We think of them as thieves, but then they say we are thieves, because the land, the rivers and the woods cannot belong to anyone." He was able to think "beyond the pale", and in his case beyond an imperial worldview that unfortunately is as powerful today as when this Italian prelate tried unsuccessfully to infiltrate the ruling groups with an eye not for the scattered communities of Ireland but for Dublin and over the sea to the most important prize, England itself. The pale is where decisions are made and agreements are brokered; beyond the pale, whether a real one or the more intangible one of intellectual independence, is where thoughts evolve free from the prejudices of power.

Being "beyond the pale" is therefore a question of viewpoint. Llorente is clearly a convinced "atheist", while I believe that God in all probability does exist (this is not the same as "believing in God", which is a certainty I cannot share and appears to distort the original meaning of the verb "to believe"). However the candour and indeed freshness of his atheism can, at least in part, be explained by his coming from a country that is dominated by what seems to us Europeans to be an insanely fanatical belief in God and the literal truth of the scriptures. We all have a different pale to move out of – a different set of certainties that need to be challenged. Not that I wish to suggest that this book is relevant only to Americans. Far from it. This is in part because Europe and America are gradually converging, and both share a rather abusive relationship with the Third World, and in part because Llorente now lives in Spain and has plenty of interesting things to say about that country and our increasingly disoriented continent.

This is a book that can be read in many different ways. You can, as I have done, read it through in a single sitting, or you can dip into it and ponder its various challenges. Or you can return to it. Today we want to do everything in a hurry, but the delight of aphorisms is that they need to be taken slowly. Their fragmentary nature means that the reader has to reconstruct the omitted parts, and each reader can do this differently. This too should – *to some extent* – be true of all literature; so this philosophical form is also essentially a literary one, and as such, we should look kindly on its reappearance in a time when publishing is fearful of "crossover" books. Crossing over the boundaries that keep us in the pale is perhaps best achieved by crossing over the boundaries that divide the way we write. Renzo Llorente has undoubtedly chosen the right genre for the bold task he has set himself.

Allan Cameron
Isle of Lewis, August 2010

Part One

I

1. It is often said that a nun, in assuming her vocation, becomes "the bride of Christ": Does that not make her the social climber par excellence? How else to regard one who *marries into the family of the Almighty*?

§

2. As we walk down any city street we are perfectly aware that all the people around us are, *underneath* their silence, carrying on endless soliloquies; yet we are hardly moved, on these grounds alone, to question their mental health. Were we to walk down the same street and find the same people carrying on their soliloquies *aloud* – exteriorizing their monologues, so to speak – we would regard each and every one of them as hopelessly deranged. To think that the differentia between sanity and madness should be a matter of *decibels*!

§

3. How to explain the inability to give *oneself* the benefit of the doubt? Whence this compulsion to *anticipate one's detractors*?

§

4. As Cioran rightly observes, "It takes an enormous humility to die. The strange thing is that everyone turns out to have it!"[1] It is equally true, of course, that the dead manage, miraculously, to *maintain* this humility. This is surely not the least of their virtues, and undoubtedly the one that most endears them to the living.

§

5. It is little wonder that people are happy to grant that so-and-so – usually a writer, thinker, political activist or the like – is the "conscience of our time": it relieves them of the responsibility of having a conscience of their own.

§

6. *Prayer as megalomania*: the believer starts a conversation with himself – and tells us that his words are addressed to *God!*

§

7. Whence the condemnation of loitering? Why this aversion to what is, after all, the definitive metaphor for "the human condition"? *To loiter*: to remain in an area for no obvious reason (Merriam-Webster).

§

8. The option of dying *while watching television*: undoubtedly the twentieth century's most remarkable innovation in the *ars moriendi*.

§

9. "Never pass up the opportunity to have sex or appear on television" (Gore Vidal). Sage counsel, to be sure; but in some sense the maxim implicit in the practice of "amateur pornography" plainly goes one better, as this activity is nothing if not a celebration of having sex and appearing on television *at one and the same time*.

§

10. To have unclear thoughts is to mumble *in silence*.

§

11. It is not easy to imagine a less interesting exercise than listening to someone else recount a dream (it is no accident that psychotherapists *charge* for this service). But why is this so? Why do we invariably find the account of another's dream insipid, no matter how absorbing it was for the one who dreamt it? The main reason, it seems, is that the *literal* account of a dream inevitably divests it of that aura of

mystery, ambiguity and opacity that the dreamer has found so bewitching. What's more, in being informed of the content of another's dream, we know from the start that the events described *were not real*, whereas the person who had the dream is relating an episode which he once took to be true, once, so to speak, lived as "real". It is, no doubt, this unreality of dreams that explains why hearing others discuss their dreams proves even more tedious than hearing them tell us how they fell in love: we know nothing of the unique mystery and opacity surrounding that experience either; yet, since it actually happened, it is in some sense as real for us as it was for them.

§

12. Those who reveal the content of their dreams engage in a kind of *genteel exhibitionism*, which is to say, exhibitionism of a socially permissible sort: just as society must provide adequate channels for the sublimated expression of other unruly impulses and desires, so, too, it must offer an outlet for acceptable manifestations of exhibitionism. What is more, assuming Freud was right, the act of casually disclosing one's dreams is actually *doubly* exhibitionistic. It is no wonder, then, that people take such obvious satisfaction in retailing the minutiae of even their most banal dreams.

§

13. Our regrets never disappoint us: no matter how regularly we frequent them, they always afford us an *inexhaustible* source of distress.

§

14. It is hard to say whether God overreacted to the mischief he discovered in the Garden of Eden, but surely there can be no doubt that as an act of collective punishment his achievement remains unsurpassed. For Yahweh's response to one man's lapse was nothing less than...*the condemnation of an entire species!*

§

15. We admire individuals possessed of moral superiority no less than we admire those whom we reckon intellectually superior or those who enjoy great power, and may even admire them more; but which people do we *envy?* The answer to this question is enough to make one despair of moral progress.

§

16. The family affords us our first taste of undesired publicity, and also acquaints us, early on, with the obligation of self-justification. Considering that such misfortunes are inherent in family life, it is more than a little surprising that a "traumatic childhood" is not the *norm.*

§

17. *Macho schizophrenia.* There is a certain kind of man who wants his girlfriend or wife to appear *conspicuously* attractive and *conspicuously* sexy, so that others will envy him, admire him, be impressed by him. In other words, he hopes that others will desire her, and expects her to dress in a way that will excite their desire. At the same time, he does *not* want others to desire her or to desire her *too much* or too openly, for he is more liable than most to feel threatened and quicker to become "defensive". In short, he hopes that others will both desire and not desire his mate at one and the same time, and hopes that she will attract their attention and not attract their attention, likewise at one and the same time. Small wonder, then, that his effect on others so resembles the apprehension that seizes us in certain encounters with the mentally ill.

§

18. We often praise optimism as though it were a virtue, when it is in fact something of a pathology. To be an optimist is to be *metaphysically* in denial.

§

19. The uniqueness of pornographic films as an art form may be most evident in their *singular conception of genre*, for often the only thing that distinguishes one genre of porn from another is *the physical appearance of the protagonists*. That is, what defines a given genre of pornography is neither the plot, nor the structure, nor the representational conventions and techniques used in a film, but rather the racial identity of the actors, or their ages, or the sizes of their bodies, or the fact that they are all of the same sex. In short, *genre* in pornography is often simply a matter of *casting*.

§

20. A lifetime of unrequited love: religions that bid us "to love God" can promise little else.

§

21. To have first turned to philosophy in the hope of finding answers to life's capital questions – *to unriddle the universe*, as Nietzsche would say – and to end one's days explaining the intricacies of ... "business ethics"!

§

22. It is odd that some deaths should be judged more worthy of – so to speak, more *qualified* for – obituaries than others, as though the one event that irrefutably demonstrates the ultimate equality – and nullity – of us all should be the very justification for undertaking a sort of final ranking. ("Your death would not even merit an obituary" would be, for this reason, no small insult.)

§

23. Perhaps the truly remarkable thing about obituaries is that, while aiming to highlight the distinctive aspects of a given life, they inevitably impoverish – and so render *less* distinctive – the life history that they describe, insofar as they simplify, distill, flatten and schematize that history. Indeed,

how many of us even recognize our relatives as they appear in the encapsulated life histories that comprise their obituaries?

§

24. It is odd that we are reluctant to draft our *own* obituaries, even taking into account the frustration in knowing that ours can never be the *definitive* version. After all, many people take great pains to reserve, if not design, a particular burial plot; some select a gravestone, including the inscription; and there are even those who make provision for their own funerals. Why, then, do most recoil from the idea of an *autobiographical* obituary?

§

25. Gargantuan malls, immense supermarkets, department stores that mock any pretension to "human scale" – the commercial institutions that surround us and define the contemporary landscape long ago renounced all efforts to appear "familiar", or to minimize their impersonal feel: *massification* is no longer burdened with a bad conscience.

§

26. "Liquor and Christianity" are, according to Nietzsche, "the European narcotics".[2] Two world wars, genocides, inquisitions, countless imperialist depredations... One shudders to think what the Old World might have accomplished *without* sedation.

§

27. Theology is the pious form of sophistry.

§

28. Viewing recent photographs of people we do not know typically leaves us indifferent, whereas it is hard to feel indifference in viewing *old* photos of people whom we do not know. (We feel less indifference still in the case of old *black-*

and-white photographs, since the poignancy produced by the passage of time is enhanced by the wondrous ability of black-and-white photography to render *everyone* photogenic.) There are various reasons for the interest aroused by old photos, regardless of our personal connection with the subject of the photograph. For one thing, old photos at least show us a world that is very different from our own, whereas photos of our contemporaries always reflect a world that is already familiar to us (it is for the same sort of reason that we find recent photos of strangers in other cultures more interesting than those of strangers from our own). For another, old photographs transmit, or rather elicit, a kind of *pathos* that is normally absent from pictures of our contemporaries: in viewing a photograph from the past we cannot fail to be aware of the ultimate *vulnerability* of the subjects presented – they may be deceased; if alive, they may be quite old, frail, sickly; if nothing else, they will, if still among the living, almost certainly appear very different today – while likely being reminded of our *own* vulnerability as well. Finally, even if this pathos is more or less absent in viewing old pictures, there remains the sheer *curiosity* that their subjects provoke, as registered in the inevitable question: *What became of them?*

§

29. When we find ourselves in a foreign land and observe any compatriots around us, we discern in addition to their personal or individual flaws their – and our – *national* short-comings. One would think, then, that only the most incurably masochistic would venture to *honeymoon* in a foreign country. Yet as it turns out...

§

30. The "occupational hazards" of astronomy: to be reminded, day in and day out, of one's utterly negligible *stature*, to see one's complete insignificance "experimentally confirmed" on a regular basis! Astronomy: the *abysmal* science.

§

31. It may seem remarkable that those who have *the least time* – old people, the elderly – have *the most patience*, but this is no doubt the true hallmark of their wisdom. Having grasped that it makes no difference in the long run whether they do one thing or another, they are indifferent to the delays that prove such a torment for the rest of us.

§

32. *Listening to oneself while talking to oneself.* The virtues of this particular mode of conversation are scarcely appreciate-ed. Consider: as a listener, you find that everything your interlocutor says is of the greatest interest to you, and that you can listen most attentively – not "miss a thing" – and remain utterly self-absorbed at one and the same time. As the one who is speaking, you find that however self-centered and solipsistic your conversation, your listener will hang on every word – in fact, the *more* self-centered your talk, the keener your listener's interest. This is indeed the only situation in which the quality of conversation – at least as far as the interest, empathy and receptivity of the listener is concerned – is actually *enhanced* by the speaker's own self-consciousness. (Perhaps, then, we should define the *absolute bore* as one who is bored by listening to himself while talking to himself.)

§

33. To die is to abandon oneself to decomposition, and this is why our *own* deaths always bring out the worst in us.

§

34. A play staged in Madrid, *Me cago en Dios* ("Screw God"; literally, "I shit on God") was, to no one's surprise, a source of lively controversy and scandal. In fact, even many unbelievers expressed sympathy for those who felt insulted by the title of the play. "Just imagine the reaction among progressive, non-religious people," remarked a friend, "if the title of the play were *To Hell with Gays* or *Screw the Jews*." At that moment I said nothing, too sluggish in my thinking to give what is, as

10

another friend later reminded me, the obvious reply: "But gays and Jews *are real.*"

§

35. Often the pleasure we take in quoting brilliant or telling dicta comes from the thrill of presenting an *unqualified* pronouncement (and, typically, one rendered in splendid language at that). Of course, contemporary intellectuals would love to be able to deliver unqualified pronouncements themselves, but their scholarly instinct and a culture that scorns sententiousness forbid them from doing so. Hence the importance, and prevalence, of this vicarious satisfaction: it allows one to pontificate *with a clean conscience.*

§

36. "Normal" behavior seems to issue from the exercise of a certain skill or talent, one which involves the ability to translate a welter of impulses, feelings, beliefs and urges into the language of *propriety.* If we bear this in mind, we shall undoubtedly display greater tolerance toward *eccentrics*: just as there are many people who do not excel at translating one spoken or written language into another, so, too, there are many who lack the skills required to render their sentiments and drives in the idiom of propriety. In a sense, then, eccentricity is simply one more variety of *incompetence in translation*; and since there is hardly any reason to condemn anyone merely for being a poor translator...

§

37. "The degree and kind of a man's sexuality reach up into the ultimate pinnacle of his spirit."[3] Nietzsche's (pre-Freudian) dictum expresses a fertile insight if there ever was one. For one thing, it goes a long way toward illuminating the resentment people feel against those who are sexually more liberated than themselves: the bondage from which others have freed themselves is precisely the form of subjugation which they suffer most acutely, its effects *reaching up into the ultimate pinnacle of their spirit.* For another, it helps to account for the

11

uneasiness that pornography – which mocks the customary association of love and sex, and liberates sex from the confines of this association – provokes in so many. It also tells us why prostitution, for all its similarities to other forms of wage-labor, intuitively strikes us as necessarily more degrading than other forms of exploitation "on the job". At the same time, it sheds light on the offense that straight people feel when mistakenly assumed to be gay. (Otherwise, a mistaken conclusion about his sexuality – "Oh, but I thought you were gay!" – ought to upset a heterosexual person no more than if someone had, say, ascribed the wrong gustatory preferences to him.) Finally, and not least of all, it provides clues as to why *bestiality* should be indignantly condemned by people who are indifferent to the far more ghastly, and ethically more reprehensible, practice of "factory farming".

§

38. Obsessions may not *build* character, but they certainly lend it *stability* and *continuity* (and often its only *momentum...*). Indeed, what better touchstone for the endurance of "personal identity" than the persistence of our obsessions?

§

39. Why do we respect the aged? Surely it is in part because we admire their *duration* and *resistance*, as Guicciardini hinted in his sixteenth-century *Maxims*: "When I consider the infinite ways in which human life is subject to accident, sickness, chance, and violence, and when I consider how many things must combine during the year to produce a good harvest, nothing surprises me more than to see an old man, a good year."[4] But just as this reflection illuminates the grounds of our reverence for the old, it also helps to explain why this reverence has long been on the wane: with modern medicine, decent nutrition, adequate hygiene, etc., sheer duration and resistance hardly merit the admiration and respect to which they were once entitled.

§

12

40. It is strange that so many are capable of cherishing their absent loved ones' personal belongings (their favorite objects, their clothes, certain mementos). One would have thought that the presence of, and the attention lavished upon, such things would serve rather to highlight or underscore the other's absence, remoteness and, in the case of death, utter *transitoriness*. What is more, my death not only annihilates me; it also annihilates the meaning of my "belongings", divesting them of the most significant relation affecting them: their value as personal, familiar possessions *for me*, things on which *I* relied, things that *I* prized. The disappearance of these relations is one of the sources of that unique emptiness we feel in roaming about the house of one who has died: the deceased's belongings suddenly appear before us destitute of some basic connection; they appear somewhat alien, and strangely out of place.

§

41. "I love the erotic spectacle but leave its staging to specialists"[5] (Salvador Dalí): surely as economical and unexceptionable a justification for pornography as has ever been written.

§

42. We are right to reckon senility and dementia the equivalent of death: to lose one's mind is to predecease *oneself.*

§

43. How is it that "to look into the other's eyes" became the hallmark, indeed the quintessential gesture, of romantic intimacy? When you truly, earnestly look into the other's eyes you see...an *organism*. One would think that the awareness of his or her – our – sheer *animality* should never be more acute, more unnerving, than when *looking into the eyes* of the loved one. But then, maybe this is but another of love's ingenious deceptions: where we ought to see a body we somehow discern a soul.

44. "There are no atheists in foxholes." How are we to explain the currency of this bizarre cliché, and the widespread belief that it actually expresses some deep truth? Or rather, how is it that foxholes are not positively *teeming with atheists*? The only sensible explanation is the corruption of intellect after millennia of exposure to religious mystification. After all, if there is one context in which the notion of an omnipotent, omnibenevolent god is simply *unthinkable*, surely it is a setting in which young men are relentlessly pulverized, forced to endure excruciating pain, maimed and mutilated for no good reason whatsoever – in a word, *in foxholes*.

§

45. "T.V. does the same thing to human relations that frozen food does to real food" (Norman Mailer).[6] No doubt this is why, at certain times, there seems to be something positively sacrilegious about turning on the television.

§

46. Socrates: the consummate *anti-bourgeois bourgeois* – as anachronistic as this may sound to some ears – that is, *the* paradigm for the "apolitical" anti-bourgeois. Always happy to shirk his duties for the ecstasies of spontaneous dialectic, Socrates was indifferent to his work, unsolicitous about his family, disdainful of any concern with dress. At the same time, his radicalism, in lifestyle as well as doctrine, abjured any attempt to alter social or political institutions – the source of *structural* constraints to virtue – and with his condemnation of all forms of civil disobedience, with his absolutist separation of ethics and politics and his individualization and decontextual-ization of all personal problems ("you must tend to your soul"!), he established that archetype for the anti-bourgeois who is tolerated, even celebrated, by the forces of order. (His fatal miscalculation at the very end is another matter.) Though it would never occur to anyone to call Wittgenstein a *Socratic* philosopher, his famous dictum to the effect that philosophy

"leaves everything as it is"[7] in fact betrays a basically Socratic outlook.

§

47. *Giving modern life its due.* "Owning a vibrator makes you glad you were born in the twentieth century" (from a manual on "sensual massage").

§

48. "A 'crowd' is the untruth," wrote Kierkegaard,[8] and he was right in more ways than one. Immersion in a crowd leads us to lose our intellectual bearings, or rather our intellectual *conscience*, and this explains that peculiar susceptibility to good oratory that we acquire on finding ourselves in the midst of a multitude. (On reading a speech that we enjoyed, we are astonished to think that we could have been moved or swayed by such trite, unnuanced rhetoric). But *why* do we lose our bearings in crowds? Surely it is because the crowd contains a *superabundance of subjectivities* (this is, of course, part of its allure), and in a space awash with so much subjectivity, *objectivity* – an essential component of intellectual conscience – barely stands a chance.

§

49. The problem with any *failure* is that it tends to summon up so many of one's previous failures; worse still, it tends to *substantiate* them. (Depression, Cioran remarks, produces a similar phenomenon: "By virtue of depression, we recall those misdeeds we buried in the depths of our memory. Depression exhumes our shames."[9])

§

50. In God's Country, religiosity *as such* is considered a virtue, and more or less automatically associated with moral rectitude; hence the contrived piety of American politicians.

§

51. In his autobiography, Lisandro Otero recounts a conversation with Graham Greene in which the latter speaks disparagingly of Somerset Maugham, among other reasons because, in his last years, Maugham "would cry like a baby when thinking that he had to die."[10] One wonders just what it is that some people find so contemptible or disgraceful in such an attitude. It is as though they believed that only those afflicted with a sickly sentimentality could possibly be unnerved by the thought that one will eventually – and in cosmic terms, *rather sooner than later* – perish forever. But what is the proper reaction to this knowledge supposed to be? Why is it not supremely *reasonable* to react as Maugham reportedly did when pondering one's own extinction?

§

52. Roland Barthes once suggested that *to know* someone is "to know his desire".[11] What, then, does it mean to be someone's *friend*? Is it not both to know that person's desire and, in a certain sense, *to share it*?

§

53. "The ancient classics are as relevant as ever": this is no doubt one of the most familiar arguments advanced by those who advocate serious attention to the classics. The trouble is, of course, that in reality time has rendered the great works of ancient literature irremediably foreign, and thus *radically irrelevant*. This is not the least of the reasons for their enduring interest, appeal, and *charm*.

§

54. Many who champion the ancient Greek classics end up insisting *both* that the beliefs, values, views, and so on that these works embody remain "relevant" – valid and applicable – today *and* that we must be careful to contextualize these works, that we must make allowances for the cultural and historical factors that distinguish the Greeks' world from ours, that we must bear in mind that the ideas expressed are linked to a specific time, place and historical experience. In other

words, they maintain at one and the same time that we must read the classics "ahistorically", and that we also must be careful *not* to read them "ahistorically".

§

55. There is undoubtedly one compelling reason to read – and take seriously – "the classics" today: they are largely immune to our contemporary ideological biases; for this reason they may prove not only instructive, but also, paradoxically, *liberating*. This is especially true of *modern* classics, for in these works we find observers who, commenting on a world that is by and large still our world today, were unconstrained by the ideological reflexes that compromise so many contemporary social analyses and who, moreover, had the advantage of seeing modern phenomena – including distinctively modern cruelties and injustices – in *simpler* forms, and thus could readily, vividly perceive many things that escape our attention, or at best appear obscure to our eyes.

§

56. Considering the degree of vindictiveness aroused by even the most insignificant affronts, why does it surprise us that ordinary people can be transformed into torturers?

§

57. Disconcerting as it is to encounter former friends who have changed so completely that they now scarcely resemble the people whose friendship we once cherished, it is even worse to encounter former friends *who have not changed at all*. Erstwhile friends of the latter sort confront us with a set of tastes and interests with which we once identified, but now find utterly foreign. In other words, their presence usually conjures up *a self that we now disown*; and as it is unnerving enough to face one's *present* self...

§

58. The relatively widespread interest in participating in "amateur pornography" should not surprise us: as a supremely *inspirational* variety of art, a pornographic film almost invariably elicits from the viewer a desire to re-enact some of its crucial sequences. (It is certainly a good thing, for society's sake, that this response is evoked by porn and not by, say, westerns.) Indeed, the hallmark of a *bad* pornographic movie is precisely that it fails to inspire you to recreate any of the actions depicted.

In any event, we will not have given "amateur pornography" its due until we have realized that it represents an unambiguous example, if not the very epitome, of *unalienated labor*, at least to the extent that the latter is possible within the constraints of capitalist societies. This is, after all, a type of work that the laborer thoroughly enjoys; that allows for and encourages free, creative self-expression; that is pursued as an end in itself; that is embraced in the absence of any coercion or financial incentive; that involves the exercise of autonomy on the job; that is performed partly out of a desire to satisfy the needs of others... (Surely not even Fourier, the most fanciful and uninhibited of the great socialist visionaries, could ever have imagined that the remedy for alienation lay in an *appeal to exhibitionism.*)

In truth, it is hard to say whether "amateur porn" reflects a complete capitulation to capitalism, or its repudiation. It is certainly true that amateur pornography in some sense involves the commodification of sexuality – after all, companies earn revenue from distributing this material – and that the performers are not even paid for their labor, and so unquestioningly consent to a kind of self-exploitation. Then again, we might just as well interpret the performers' indifference to remuneration as a commitment to satisfying the needs of others *because* they are the needs of others and *therefore* ought to be satisfied, which amounts to a rejection of capitalist values.

§

59. We know that we have reached the pinnacle of vanity when the only criticism that we are still willing to consider is *self*-criticism.

60. "Die at the right time – thus teaches Zarathustra. ... My death I praise to you, the free death which comes to me because *I* want it. And when shall I want it? He who has a goal and an heir will want death at the right time for his goal and heir."[12] No doubt Nietzsche's actual demise provides the definitive gloss on this passage, while at the same time confirming that he was, until the very end, nothing if not *the* master parodist.

§

61. Interviewed on her way to a presidential inauguration, where she was to take her place alongside hundreds of thousands of other spectators, a woman speaks of her desire to "be a part of history". It is a telling statement, as it attests to the currency of the consumer view of life, with its mystification and celebration of passivity. How else could a witness to history, a mere onlooker, mistake herself for one of its protagonists?

§

62. *Uniforms* depersonalize or "de-individuate" those who wear them (this is of course true by definition). Depersonalization, in turn, produces a dissolution of moral responsibility, for we cannot clearly identify, "single out", who is responsible for an act. Hence the peculiar arrogance and aggressiveness of many police officers, security guards and so on: at one and the same time they are vested with power and authority, *and* freed of much of their moral responsibility. (The additional legal impunity that they may enjoy is of course a separate question.)

§

63. Why exactly are we supposed to be "respectful" of others' religious beliefs? No matter how outlandish, illogical, childish, and downright *silly* another's religious convictions,

we are expected to treat them with respect – but why? What is so special about *this* form of superstition?

§

64. Undoubtedly the best one-liner from Heidegger – a charlatan for the most part, to be sure, nonpareil as a purveyor of "deeply significant nonsense" (A.J. Ayer) – is his remark that "Language is the house of Being."[13] One implication of Heidegger's remark, and certainly of the related notion that language profoundly conditions one's comprehension and *assimilation* of the world and thus the configuration of one's personal identity, is that by speaking another language, one in effect assumes another identity. We see some confirmation of this in the way that one's personality emerges or takes shape in and through another language, owing to the familiar constraints and limitations on self-expression. By the same token, we *sound* the same in a foreign language only insofar as we speak the language poorly; the greater our mastery of a (non-native) second language, the greater the distance from the tone and style that we display in speaking in our native tongue. Hence our sense that *imposture* is to some extent inevitable when speaking a foreign language. (Naturally, the strategies or habits that we use to compensate for certain linguistic inadequacies are also a factor here, i.e. they, too, inevitably engender a certain sense of imposture, at least on some occasions.)

§

65. A sage is one whose "gut reaction" comes from the *head*.

§

66. According to Schopenhauer, music "reproduces all the emotions of our innermost being," for it "expresses ... the inner being, the in-itself, of the world, which we think of under the concept of will."[14] Schopenhauer's theory tells us, among other things, why music can prove so affecting and exert such power over us when we listen to it while *alone*: we experience that

20

sense of self-transcendence – music links us to "the inner being ... of the world" and thus others within the world – which is normally only a possibility when we find ourselves in the company of others; which is to say, we experience at once both the pathos of solitude *and* the pathos of self-transcendence. Schopenhauer's theory also explains why music serves as such an effective medium for the transmission of *political* messages: at the same time as it moves us personally (in both a crudely sensorial way and insofar as it "reproduces all the emotions of our innermost being"), music also evokes, accentuates and *exploits* our sense of connection with others.

§

67. In 2000, an Italian Cardinal revealed that the Antichrist is now busily promoting vegetarianism and environmentalism. To think that *even the Antichrist* is powerless to withstand that relentless banalization to which the Church itself succumbed so many years ago...

§

68. When others find us in the act of reproaching ourselves for some minor failing or misdeed, they often assure us, by way of consolation, "You're being too hard on yourself." That is to say, "There is no need for you to be as hard on yourself as you would be on anyone else."

§

69. *The Land of the Free.* If there really is an experience or atmosphere of "freedom" peculiar to the United States, the freedom in question is plainly not, as many would have us believe, some unique manifestation of *political* freedom, but rather a freedom of an *existential* sort: the freedom for self-invention and self-*reinvention*. Indeed, nowhere is one freer to remake and recreate oneself, no questions asked, than in the US. It is, of course, easier to negotiate the collective past when one lives in a young nation, and this is one reason why in the United States personal identity is less freighted with, or less

21

constrained by, history (including family and community history). But there are other aspects of the American Way of Life which also prove particularly conducive to freedom for self-invention: the exceptional geographical and occupational mobility – work and locale both condition personal identity – that is characteristic of life in the United States and, no less important, the frenetic quality of American capitalism, which, with its relentless reordering of the social landscape and incessant erasure of history, likewise facilitates the construction of new identities. It is therefore no surprise that immigrants – people who willy-nilly *must* reinvent themselves – often find American society most congenial, or that the renascence of the "born again" should almost invariably occur within the United States.

§

70. The dead are, sad to say, all alike: the trauma of extinction renders everyone a conformist.

§

71. It is hard not to believe that there is something positively *immoral* in the conduct of the person who *bores* us. Not only does the bore divest us of our time; he also increases the volume of boredom in the world, as if convinced that humanity suffers from a shortage of this particular evil. Of course, it is also hard not to believe that the *disposition to bore others* affords a certain measure of "survival value" or some kind of "evolutionary advantage". The rather alarming incidence of this particular trait can hardly be explained otherwise.

§

72. Indifference to the fact of one's own mortality: is this not the *ne plus ultra* of "false consciousness"?

§

73. Accustomed to such informality in our own personal letters, we find the formality in letters from the past as astonishing as it is amusing. In fact, we now automatically equate intimacy with extreme informality – indeed, it has in some sense become *the* token of intimacy. Nietzsche: "[T]he style and spirit of letters will always be the true 'sign of the times'."[15]

§

74. *Porn* stardom is of course a peculiarly contemporary phenomenon, but the porn star is perhaps above all the quintessential *postmodern celebrity*. For the porn star belongs to a genre that scrambles the customary high-culture/low-culture associations, in that pornography (or at least the type of porn that yields *stars*) is at once both popular and esoteric. Even more important, the porn star's celebrity presupposes a blurring of the public/private divide, or rather a wholly new relationship between these two spheres. This is true, for one thing, because the genesis of celebrity in this case is essentially private, the porn star's performances – the grounds for his or her claim to stardom – almost never being viewed by more than a few people at a time, all of whom are typically on intimate terms with one another. In short, the star's (public) celebrity arises from an aggregation of essentially private activities. To be sure, the same thing might be said of, say, the celebrity of novelists. Yet unlike famous novelists, porn stars attain celebrity status even though the people to whom they owe this status – the fans of porn actors and actresses and the films in which they appear – are normally unwilling to acknowledge publicly their contribution to, or even familiarity with, the stars' celebrity status. This is also what distinguishes their fame from that of "mainstream" actors. When it is a matter of Hollywood productions or even "underground" work, we acknowledge which movies we have seen, enthusiastically discuss scenes from the films that we have enjoyed, and readily offer our opinion on different actors' assets or the merits and weaknesses of their various performances. This seldom happens, however, in connection with pornographic films. In any case, the essential "postmodernity" of the porn stars' celebrity is also evident in the fact that contemporary

23

pornography epitomizes "total publicity", for there can hardly be any concept more suitable for referring to *close-ups of a person's genitals*. Lastly, the most important media for viewing pornography today, and hence for the production of porn stardom, are video, DVDs and the Internet, and these are, needless to say, media proper to the postmodern era.

§

75. We perform a tedious job that requires sustained concentration: we *squander consciousness*.

§

76. One reason that we sense the "datedness" of recent socio-historical writings even more keenly than that of the old classics is that we ourselves have participated in, or rather lived through, the advent and dissolution of the very circumstances treated in the more recent works. That is, we were witness to their very evanescence – indeed, it was an immediate, concrete experience for us. To the extent that this is so (and especially to the extent that we are aware of our own *identification* with these past, extinct circumstances), recent junctures retain a particular specificity for us, and for this reason we feel the absence of these circumstances more acutely. On the other hand, of course, we are aware of *what is missing* from more recent works, whereas we can never reach a comparable awareness of what is missing from works that explore an era of which we have no first-hand experience.

§

77. It is seldom noticed that the attitude of Rodin's "Le Penseur" is in fact much more typical of children than adults (just think, for instance, of a bored or dejected child sitting alone on a step or curb). The irony of this fact is appreciated less often still.

§

78. To be sure, the problem with categorical hostility to "religion" is that one lumps together and condemns *in toto* the most disparate phenomena connected with religious practices and institutions: thus one dismisses in the same breath both the Spanish Inquisition and valuable ethical precepts; both dogmatic theology and a natural yearning for self-transcendence, or communion with others in the face of our common doom; both American-style television evangelism and the most enlightened deism; both reactionary Islamic theocracy and Liberation Theology. Of course, to acknowledge the "positive" side of religion is hardly to excuse the utter dearth of *creativity* when it comes to fashioning new gods. (Nietzsche: "Almost two thousand years – and not a single new god!"[16])

§

79. There is nothing mysterious about our distaste for *outspoken* nihilists: they confront us with a *pedantic lucidity*, which we naturally regard as the one unforgivable form of pedantry.

§

80. The rigors of solitude are not what they used to be, if only on account of the ubiquity of telecommunications media, which have taken the *edge* off solitude. (Silence, Antonio Machado once observed, is "the acoustic side of nothingness".[17]) To be "alone" with a stereo or television at one's disposal is hardly comparable to a solitude without either of these amenities; and an experience of solitude in the most desolate country setting today may include these things and even more (e.g. the Internet). All the same, despite these changes it seems clear that our *threshold* for solitude is, like our capacity to withstand the ravages of this condition, far lower than it was in the past.

§

81. *The geometry of intimacy.* If you want to know whether your relationship with another person is "intimate" in nature, you need only ask yourself whether or not you have *lain down*

beside that person, or could lie beside her (as is the case with lovers, some relatives and certain close friends), without this striking either one of you as "awkward", "unusual" or "strange". You need only ask yourself, in other words, if your relationship allows for *horizontal encounters*.

§

82. To indulge in tourism is to practice a kind of *public dilettantism*, which is why the tourist is by far the least discreet of dilettantes.

§

83. We often encounter people who have a *political* opinion of a politician, despite knowing virtually nothing at all about the actual content and implications of the politician's views. Such an opinion is in effect the epitome of *groundless belief*, based as it is on image alone – i.e. *appearance*. While these sorts of opinions have no doubt always existed, modern media, starting with photography, have surely increased their incidence and influence, at the same time as they seem to have enhanced their psychological allure. In short, groundless belief *flourishes in post-Enlightenment culture*, and so affords us still further proof, along with the contemporary currency of religious superstition, that the Enlightenment was plainly much more successful in fostering *tolerance* than it was in promoting *rationality*.

§

84. It is no wonder that we find insomnia so disquieting, a sign that something is terribly amiss in the depths of one's soul. After all, how can it be possible to lack *an aptitude for sleep*?

§

85. If the allure of religion continues to prove irresistible for so many of our contemporaries, it is in large measure thanks to the exceptional *permissiveness* of religious milieux: where

else is one allowed to utter banalities and falsehoods publicly, without the slightest fear of ridicule or reproach? Indeed, religions positively encourage us to voice ideas that are by turns insipid and insane – "convictions" in religious parlance – with the utmost solemnity and, most important, guarantee that we can always count on a respectful, sympathetic hearing for these ideas. Those who criticize the "intolerance" of religions thus usually miss the point. The problem is not that religions are intolerant, but that they tolerate all the wrong things.

§

86. It is bad enough that death happens to *other* people. That *we* are not spared, either, is simply intolerable.

§

87. Is *expatriation*, or at least anything more than a very partial, qualified expatriation, even a *possibility* for an American today? After all, the ubiquity of American products, the de facto universality of American culture (in the sense both that it is found everywhere, and that it represents a blend of so many disparate cultures), the status of English as the "international" language – do not all of these factors, along with ever-present access to "American life", conspire to render the notion of expatriation meaningless when applied to Americans living abroad?

§

88. The chief virtue of moving about foreign lands? The *mundane* never loses its novelty.

§

89. As we age, we typically become more tolerant or charitable concerning the foibles, frailties and mistakes of *individuals*, while becoming less tolerant as regards those of *society* as a whole. We seem, that is, to become more tolerantly *pluralist* regarding the individuals we encounter, readier to

accept even people with antithetical ideas, values, convictions, lifestyles and so on, while at the same time we prove less and less willing to exhibit the same benevolence and generosity toward society, and increasingly incapable of enduring *its* shortcomings (or at any rate, its divergence from our vision – typically based in part on the past we knew – of what it ought to be). This is one reason – the distinction and opposition between politics and ethics being another – that it is not unusual to find older people who have become more "liberal" in their moral outlook and yet politically more "conservative".

§

90. A reliance on print media and radio as sources of information, combined with a limitation on one's exposure to television – i.e. *televised* – news, surely facilitates the ability to think historically in at least one respect: in the mind of the person who obtains her information mainly from radio and/or the press, the disjunction between a vague, abstract, more or less indeterminate past and the rich, vivid, concrete, absolutely *real* present is likely to be less pronounced, since the bulk of her information about, and understanding of, both past *and* present is derived from non-visual sources. She will, consequently, find it easier to understand and experience historical development as a *continuum,* which is to say, she will be better prepared for thinking historically.

§

91. To think that one can point to no *hobby* other than relentless self-dissection!

§

92. One of the many reasons why we find the sight of the poor unsettling is that their situation reminds us of our own vulnerability to the passage of time. Unable to afford *new* things – things that have not yet been touched (let alone *eroded*) by temporality – the poor are typically surrounded by objects that reflect the ravages of time: threadbare clothing, worn-out furniture, antiquated appliances and gadgets, old

radios and televisions, dilapidated houses, cars on the verge of collapse... Most of their belongings, most of the things that frame and structure their existence, evoke and attest to the passing of time – something that we prefer not to acknowledge, and strive to forget.

§

93. Our uneasiness at the sight of the poor has important implications for environmental thought. As is well known, part of consumer society's power of seduction is due to its success in creating the illusion of an eternal present: we are plied with goods that are new, clean, untouched by the passage of time. Yet the creation of an ecologically sustainable society will of course require, among other things, that we curb our desires and needs for such goods, which means that we shall have to accustom ourselves to wearing, using, owning and living among things that appear more *time*worn (from cups and shopping bags to appliances and cars). For many this will seem, at least in the beginning, to entail a considerable material impoverishment, and this is, indeed, one reason that the creation of an ecologically-oriented society will prove such a daunting task. But *habituation to the timeworn* – which is but one aspect of the requisite *dishabituation to extreme abundance* – also involves another, completely different sort of problem. If consumer society, with its fabrication (in every sense of the word) of an eternal present, obscures or conceals our mortality, the obligation to make do with *aged* goods cannot but remind us of *our own* subjection to time, and the fact that *we* do not escape its withering passage, either. Which is to say, the prevalence of timeworn goods will make it more difficult for us to ignore or deny our own mortality.

§

94. The real enigma of mysticism is the extreme *modesty* of most mystics: *blessed* with such gifts, why would any mystic in her right mind limit herself to *one* god?

§

95. *Independent Scholar.* In today's academy-centered intellectual culture, this label often functions in much the same way as "autodidact" did in the past: it tends to prompt a kind of *a priori* skepticism about the reliability, solidity and authority of both the author and her ideas.

§

96. *Perennial Puritanism.* The major US Supreme Court decisions bearing on obscenity have used "prurience" or "appeal to prurient interest", as one of the definitive criteria in determining whether or not a particular work is to be considered obscene. Judging by the Court's arguments and commentary, and the sort of works invariably classified as "obscene" (notably "hard-core" pornography), one can only conclude that for the justices the essence of "prurience" is something like *a keen interest in sex for its own sake.* Yet what exactly is wrong with *that?* In a country still saturated with puritanism, it is assumed that there is simply no need to pose this question, let alone answer it.

§

97. Suicide is an extreme act, to be sure, not least of all because of its utter *superfluousness.*

§

98. On at least one occasion during his presidency, Bill Clinton invoked the television "sitcoms" of the 1950s by way of conjuring up his vision of the model American family. It was of course, as many pointed out at the time, an utterly fatuous gesture, for even if such domestic arrangements were a desirable ideal, contemporary economic realities have made them an impossibility for most Americans. The real significance of the President's reference, however, lay elsewhere, namely in the fact that it illustrated the degree to which the United States has become a completely television-referential culture, and that television's images are now regarded as a kind of historical record (independent of television): i.e. people regard them not as, say, normative models, but rather as

general historical documents in their own right, records of "non-televisual" or "extra-televisual" reality. In other words, they are perceived as records of history as such, instead of records – documents – of *television* history, or at most partial reflections of, or clues to, larger historical realities.

§

99. "Old folks' homes", "nursing homes", "geriatric care facilities"...: what do these institutions offer if not an *apprenticeship for death*? How else to describe the experience of the "patients" and "residents" who, having already endured the onset of their own *obsolescence*, are progressively *weaned from life*?

§

100. The enviable status – indeed, part of the romance – of the student derives as much from her freedom from a fixed role as from her freedom from countless "adult" responsibilities. While still a student, her fate remains highly indeterminate; she has yet to assume the identity and attendant delimitation that one incurs by assuming a given occupational role. To be sure, to be a student is to have a role of sorts; however, unlike typical occupational roles, the role of the student is ill-defined (due to the inclusiveness of the term and the fact that students are preparing themselves for all sorts of roles) and supposed to be transitory. Consequently, her identity remains unusually amorphous: she can still, and undoubtedly will, evolve into something, someone else. On the other hand, once we assume a particular position or career, establish a family and so on, our horizon of possibilities contracts dramatically: in a word, we are domesticated.

§

101. Satisfaction at the death of another: the supreme expression of *Schadenfreude*.

§

31

102. How is it that Freud could so thoroughly neglect the activity of prayer? Society indulges and even fosters the conceit that one can carry on a tête-à-tête with the Creator – what better method for containing, through sublimation, the irrepressible urge to self-aggrandizement? All the same, while the invention of prayer remains unsurpassed in this respect, Freud appears to ignore the topic entirely in his reflections on religion.

§

103. Is it really any wonder that one should prefer solitude, given how easy it is *to discredit oneself* thoroughly – not least of all in one's own eyes – in front of others?

§

104. As happens with a language in which we are not completely at home, a foreign currency can only strike us as something of a contrivance; lacking the transparency of *our* representation of value, its utter *arbitrariness* appears patent, palpable...

§

105. We approximate *pure* states of consideration, respect and compassion for others only when visiting a cemetery, listening to a eulogy, reading an obituary, attending a funeral, etc.; in other words, only when the "others" in question are *extinct,* and therefore incapable of feeling, perceiving or doing anything at all. This is a particularly impressive testimony to the power of the dead: despite their impotence, they somehow manage to elicit from us a measure of selflessness and solicitude that we would never dream of extending to the living.

§

106. It is rather surprising that *chronic paranoia* is not far more prevalent among the faithful, most of whom live day after day with the conviction that there exists an omniscient being

who is both keenly interested in their affairs and ready to pass judgment on their lives. Then again, perhaps we should simply view their capacity to entertain this conviction without succumbing to paranoia as proof that, as many believers themselves are wont to say, faith "gives them strength".

§

107. If proselytizers are a menace to society, it is in part because, with their agitprop activity on behalf of the Almighty, they contribute to *fomenting paranoia*, a practice which a more enlightened society would naturally regard as the height of social irresponsibility.

§

108. We have a unique link to those whose lifetimes happen to overlap with our own, that is, with those who are assigned *to people our fate*. They are the only human beings whom we shall ever have the chance to know, communicate with, observe, etc.; and to the extent that we ever experience genuine feelings of *existential solidarity*, these people will be both the inspiration and beneficiary of this sentiment. Whence the *pathos of contemporaneity*.

§

109. That society as a whole (and not just, say, its intellectuals) has assimilated the equation of *modernity* with increasing differentiation is evident from the success of advertising, and marketing in general. Pseudo-differentiation among virtually identical products succeeds in large part because *any* differentiation seems to be a token of modernization and modernity, and hence an improvement, an advance – in a word, *something better*.

§

110. "I'm an American!" exclaimed the man at the airport, in protesting the rather indifferent treatment and unconsoling explanations that he was receiving from airline authorities and

security personnel. (Along with many others, he had been stranded in the airport because of a major snowstorm.) Surely one does not hear comparable affirmations ("But I'm a German!" or "I'm Brazilian!") with the same frequency among people of other nations – ardent nationalists aside – let alone, as is so often the case with the protestation that one is an American, *outside their own countries*. Indeed, Americans are probably unique in thinking that their national status should entitle them to special rights and privileges even in other lands. But whatever one thinks of this mindset, one can hardly deny its power of seduction: the man at the airport was, to all appearances, a *Dominican-American*, and he shouted "I'm an American!" in heavily accented English.

§

111. Epictetus: "When you are about to meet someone, especially someone who seems to be distinguished, put to yourself the question, 'What would Socrates or Zeno have done in these circumstances?'"[18] Follow the example of a *Socrates*? Would Epictetus really have us emulate a man whose inclinations led him to *humiliate* "distinguished" persons, and whose continual affronts to such people were ultimately rewarded with a death sentence? Whatever wisdom Socrates may have possessed, he was anything but *worldly-wise*, a fact which should hardly have been lost on the great Stoic Epictetus.

§

112. Nowadays one occasionally comes across amateur publicity ploys that use the phrase "Free Sex!" to attract people's attention. (The next line is in fact often *"Now that we've got your attention..."*) The efficacy of this ploy is revealing, for it essentially confirms that most people believe that we normally *do not* get sex "for nothing", that usually some sort of cost is associated with getting it, that typically we must make a significant sacrifice in order to experience sex, that somehow we almost always have to *work* for it (perhaps even if we are married). The efficacy of the "Free Sex!" ads thus

affords us more insight into the prevailing sexual ethos than any number of sexological treatises.

§

113. As far as the relevance of contemporary, academic political philosophy to real-world politics is concerned, we could hardly do better than to paraphrase a quip by Marx and Engels in *The German Ideology*: "Philosophy and the study of the actual world have the same relation to one another as onanism and sexual love."[19]

§

114. *Decency.* Is this not the lingua franca of morality?

§

115. The dead are indeed so many "extinct subjectivities", as Maurice Merleau-Ponty once put it.[20] Hence the aim and task of history, and especially biography – *the history of a subjectivity* – must be the *revival* of these subjectivities, i.e. the restoration of the richness, the dynamism, the existential density, the *pathos* of a living subjectivity. This is one reason why historical works (e.g. biographies) *without pictures* – photographs, paintings, sketches, whatever – do such a disservice to history: rather than helping us to "relate" and link our own history to the figures and events they describe or represent, rather than aiding us in minimizing the inevitable psychological and epistemological incommensurability that hampers our efforts to absorb the past, such works actually tend to reinforce the irreducible *abstractness* of history, devaluing the importance of the visual and sensory experience of actions, events, encounters, crises, conflicts, etc. The result is that the lives and times of our predecessors appear either as fundamentally impoverished (less vibrant, rich and dynamic than our own) or as totally remote from – and unrelated to – our own, or both.

§

116. We should not forget that *historical alienation* – the incapacity to "relate to" or attach importance to the past, our psychological remoteness from the passions and sensibilities that shaped our ancestors' lives – facilitates the work of those who *exploit the past*, distorting history or representing it in a tendentious fashion: if many can barely conceive of the past and are at any rate indifferent to it, propagandists find much of their work already done for them.

§

117. Ever fewer all-embracing theories, a diminishing tolerance for sweeping generalizations, more and more extreme micro-specialization: recent intellectual history affords us a record of *increasing human humility*, which is undoubtedly the reason why we find it *unique*.

§

118. Perhaps we should not judge "organized religion" so severely; perhaps it's simply the case that most people need a *pretext*, or at any rate a *prompt*, for an experience of rapturous self-transcendence. All the same, must the prompt really be so very *crude*?

§

119. One problem with the video camera, or rather its ubiquity, is that it hinders the activity that Nietzsche calls "active forgetfulness" which, he wrote, "is like a doorkeeper, a preserver of psychic order, repose, and etiquette: so that it will be immediately obvious how there could be no happiness, no cheerfulness, no hope, no pride, no *present*, without forgetfulness. The man in whom this apparatus of repression is damaged and ceases to function properly may be compared …with a dyspeptic – he cannot 'have done' with anything."[21] Then again, perhaps the problem is not so much the video camera's impact on this operation as on a correlative activity, namely *creative remembering*. For just as we *need* forgetfulness, we also need to *remember after our own fashion*. Whereas photos, the very embodiment of *stasis*, serve as a mere prompt

for memory, and so allow it considerable latitude, video artifacts, and for that matter all *filmed* records of social gatherings, ceremonies, trips, celebrations and so on, hamper the creative activity of memory, its efforts to embellish, distort, accentuate and reconfigure certain features of past experiences so as to render them manageable and assimilable or, at the very least, *bearable*.

§

120. Recent technological advances, especially insofar as they result in an increasing technologicization of leisure and recreation, have no doubt exacerbated the United States' endemic anti-intellectualism: the burden of diversion is shifting more and more to the machine, the device, the gadget...

§

121. In the preface to one of her books, a foreign-born philosopher who lives and teaches in the United States writes, by way of acknowledging financial support from a European institution, of an "old-world commitment and generosity toward the study of the humanities".[22] It is a telling remark: just as less sophisticated immigrants absorb the native prejudices as part of their "assimilation", so immigrant intellectuals assume their American counterparts' uninformed disparagement of American philistinism. (However anti-intellectual American society as a whole may be, today's old-world universities fare rather badly when their "commitment and generosity toward the study of the humanities" is compared with their American counterparts, as someone who has spent time in old-world universities ought to know.)

§

122. It is curious that trite poetry or song lyrics (and many other banalities) which we hear and understand in a foreign language strike us as far more profound, far more memorable, than if we heard them rendered in our native tongue. No doubt the reason for this is that the "foreign" words retain an

inevitable opacity for us, which arouses a certain wonder, whether or not we also mistake this opacity for a unique emotional or conceptual depth.

§

123. In a rare interview at the time of his "trial" and so only shortly before his execution, Pol Pot was keen to set the record straight: *No!*, contrary to the claim made by one of his biographers, he had not been a "mediocre" student...[23]

§

124. To be sure, "the unexamined life is not worth living", but *how* are we supposed to examine our lives? Presumably the aim is to examine our lives with some measure of objectivity, but this is seldom possible and, in any case, can only result in paralysis. Hence our dilemma: the unexamined life is not worth living, and the examined life proves *unlivable*. Fortunately, each of us excels at scrutinizing the lives of *others*; and thus we ensure that everyone's life is examined in exhaustive detail, and with an objectivity whose severity could hardly be surpassed.

§

125. As befits a people with such a "practical" bent, the US is a nation *obsessed with methodology*. Hence the success of "How-To" books, the popularity of "personal improvement" programs, the fixation on the minutiae of method in theories of pedagogy, and so on.

§

126. Descartes: "Reading good books is like a conversation with the noblest people of past centuries – their authors – indeed, even a studied conversation in which they discover only the best of their thoughts."[24] Maybe so – but what a queer notion of "conversation"!

§

38

127. Normally we divulge our superstitions only with great reluctance and more than a hint of shame. Yet we sometimes hear believers tell us how *proud* they are of their "faith", as though adherence to some extravagant creed justified a certain religious self-conceit. It is perfectly understandable, of course, that people should embrace superstition sooner than resign themselves to their own ultimate annihilation. But why should this be a source of *pride*?

§

128. If we are unhappy with the impression that we make on someone whom we have met for the first time and shall probably never see again, the thought that this is also the *last* time that we will see that person is supposed to be a source of great consolation, even liberating. Hence the friend's typical reaction: "What do you care what he thinks of you? You'll never see him again in your life." But is such lack of concern really well founded? Or rather, should we not worry about the other's opinion for the very reason that *we'll never see him again* (and *he'll never see us again*)? Whereas we can always try to rectify or remedy a bad impression that we may have made on those whom we see frequently or at least more than once, in the case of the person whom we meet once and shall never see again we normally have but a single opportunity to shape his opinion of us. Accordingly, if there is one sort of person whose opinion really ought to matter to us...

§

129. Why bemoan, as some do, the interest we take in authors' lives (as opposed to their works)? After all, the lives of talented, successful writers often possess the same charm and appeal as those of aristocrats and celebrities: a freedom and remoteness from *the exigencies of the daily grind*, regular contact with interesting, colorful companions, and abundant opportunities for adventure of one sort or another. And if the account of a writer's life is autobiographical to boot, our interest in her life exposes us to her work; that is to say, it leads us to take an interest in the author's *writing*.

§

130. Cioran: "There are a thousand perceptions of Nothing, and only one word to translate them: the indigence of language renders the universe intelligible..."[25] Indeed: the certitude of nothingness is overdetermined.

§

131. *Living in the past.* Why should this be reckoned a failing when it is a matter of a more or less remote past, yet unobjectionable when it is a matter of the immediate past (say, last week)? It is usually the case, to be sure, that the immediate past bears on our present and near future in a way and with a forcefulness that the remote past does not. But whenever this is not the case, then what we have is simply another glaring "asymmetry" regarding time perception.

In any case, whatever our view of nostalgics, it would seem to be more *rational*, in some sense, to be "living in the past" than to be "living in the *future*", for something that once occurred but is no longer is certainly more *real* than something that may well occur in the future but has not yet occurred. In short, what happened in the past has at least *been real* at one time, and so if it is more rational to commit oneself to things that are *more* real rather than those that are *less* real...

§

132. Schopenhauer famously decried *noise* as a menace to thought, which it invariably disturbs and interrupts. (He himself was particularly exercised by the crack of whips.) Schopenhauer could of course hardly have foreseen the astronomical increase in noise – from automobile traffic, the use of machinery, regular encroachments from others' musical entertainment, etc. – in the century and a half after his death, or that we would eventually be justified in identifying late modernity with the *universalization of noise*. Yet his strictures doubtless remain relevant today, at least to the extent that our thinking appears rather sterile as compared with that of earlier generations: part of the problem may be *too much noise*. (On

40

the other hand, Schopenhauer's view also implies that our thinking will actually *improve* once we establish more ecological societies, assuming that such societies succeed in reducing the level of "noise pollution" in the world.)

§

133. What is history if not *time anthropomorphized*?

§

134. One reason for the exaltation of the *critic* in recent literary theory: the sterility of contemporary literary production is such that critics no longer appear any less *creative* than the authors whom they study.

§

135. If religious commitment ought to be rooted in faith, a *serious* religion will admit only those converts whose conversion is the product of revelation, for a conversion wrought by proselytism or one that issues from a careful consideration of the merits and flaws of different doctrines is a conversion based on rational deliberation, which is of course completely antithetical to the faith of religious conviction. (How many devout parents encourage their children to assess the strengths and weaknesses of rival religious views?) In short, a "rational conversion" makes reason, the proverbial nemesis of religion, the source of one's conviction, and thereby taints, corrupts and menaces this conviction from the start. A conversion prompted by revelation, on the other hand, yields a faith that is both free of all rational contamination and essentially immune to any kind of rational critique, in that it enjoys the sort of metaphysical justification and authority that we associate with a deep, intuitive truth. Indeed, the convictions of a believer whose faith derives from this type of conversion can only be shaken by... a subsequent revelation.

§

136. Max Weber on *the pathos of specialization*: "Only by strict specialization can the scientific worker become fully conscious, for once and perhaps never again in his lifetime, that he has achieved something that will endure. A really definitive and good accomplishment is today always a specialized accomplishment. And whoever lacks the capacity to put on blinders, so to speak ... may as well stay away from science."[26] To think that Weber made this pronouncement in 1918! Farsighted as Weber was, it is hard to imagine that he could ever have foreseen the dimensions of the blinders, so to speak, that the specialist must wear today.

§

137. Why is it that self-contempt should be experienced as a distressing condition? After all, to feel contempt for oneself is to feel contempt for the one who feels contempt. But if I feel contempt for the one who feels contempt, if I am contemptuous of the person *whose contempt it is*, what reason is there for me to attach any importance to this contempt? Since we would normally not respect or attach much importance to the opinion of someone for whom we feel contempt, why should it be any different in this case? Why, in short, can we not accept that self-contempt "cancels itself out"?

§

138. "Philosophy ... is *its own time comprehended in thoughts*" (Hegel).[27] What is *nihilism*, then, if not the *expiration* of one's *own* time comprehended in thoughts?

§

139. As far as the prospects for "religious" insight today are concerned, perhaps Timothy Leary was right in claiming that the depth of our alienation and desensitization today is such that for most people nothing short of the jolt delivered by psychedelic drugs will suffice to make truly religious insight and experience possible. Even for those with a strong inclination to such experience (i.e. those who naturally tend to

a "spiritual" or religious awareness and appreciation of the world), the traditional methods for facilitating spiritual enlightenment – meditation, contemplation, prayer and the performance of certain intellectual or physical exercises – promise little efficacy. Our times apparently demand a more potent tonic, a more *brutal* technique, and psychedelic drugs, with their power to produce a certain *desecration of the everyday world*, seem to fit the bill.

§

140. A dog is dressed in a sweater, a rabbit is wearing glasses, two chimpanzees are shown smoking cigarettes and sipping beer... Why is it that animals appear so degraded when we outfit them with the trappings of homo sapiens, or when we show them engaged in distinctively "human" activities?

§

141. E.P. Thompson rightly lamented "the enormous con-descension of posterity."[28] What he neglected to add is that, insofar as such condescension taints, to one degree or another, just about *everyone*'s apprehension of *all things past*, this is due partly to the perceived *deficiency* of all earlier times – as Ortega y Gasset suggested – and partly to the relative "naivety" and "ignorance" (human knowledge is cumulative...) of those who came before us. ("What a limited world they inhabited?" "How could they have taken such things so seriously?" "How could they possibly have felt such an attachment to *those* practices and institutions?")

But then, how many of us are really ready to believe that within a few hundred years no one, apart from a handful of specialist historians, will appreciate any *qualitative* differences in social life between, say, 1955 and 1995? For distant posterity, the crucial generational differences that define our identity and so fascinate us will in all likelihood be imperceptible, just as we ourselves are blind to the transform-ations in cultural sensibility separating, say, 1658 from 1618. Future generations will simply have no inkling of, or at any rate feeling for – let alone interest in – the *pathos of our time*, to say nothing of the particular cultural and psychological divides to which we attach such importance.

§

142. The major monotheistic religions, with their eschatological fables, *trivialize death*. Is this not reason enough to spurn them?

§

143. "Power tends to corrupt; absolute power corrupts absolutely." If Acton's famous dictum is true, the danger of excessive individual freedom proves less of an enigma, since freedom consists, in large part, of *power over oneself*; indeed, to the extent that freedom is akin to *autonomy*, it is little else. More freedom, then, means more power, and so an increase in the former will, if Acton is right, tend to corrupt us. It turns out, then, that there is good reason for limiting one's *power over oneself* and, correlatively, for embracing the paradoxical *virtue of disempowerment*.

§

144. Few people believe that friendship between people of radically different *moral* outlooks is possible – what morally respectable person would claim an immoralist as a friend? How is it, then, that two people of antithetical political views can be *friends*? Perhaps everything depends on the extent to which political differences are related to, or rooted in, moral differences. But even if we suppose that there is in principle no necessary connection between politics and ethics, there still seems to be something strange about the idea that two people of antithetical political views can be *friends*. For to say that political differences need not matter is to suggest that the convictions, principles, values and commitments that shape an individual's political outlook need not shape her personal identity, and hence need not affect her relations with other people. This might be true in the case of people who do not take politics very seriously; but what about those who do?

Perhaps political differences are important, then, only when a friend's views issue in action, i.e. when the friend whose views run counter to one's own is politically active. But if this is right, what is to stop one from maintaining friendships with, say, apolitical Nazis?

Perhaps the answer to this question is to be found in the public/private dichotomy, or in the fact that *existential* solidarity usually trumps *political* solidarity, or even in a simple recognition of our own fallibility... Then again, maybe it is simply the case that friendships can, and in some sense should, accommodate almost *anything*, and that this is, indeed, the real enigma and appeal of friendship.

Part Two

Part Two

II

1. Many of the plastic dog turds sold in the US are, it turns out, manufactured in China. That we import such products – and all the way from *China*, no less – is more than a little intriguing: is it really necessary to have plastic turds *imported*? And one wonders just what the Chinese workers themselves are thinking, as they watch these handsomely packaged plastic turds come tumbling off the conveyor belt. In beholding such a sight, even the most cynical among them no doubt come to the conclusion that there was something to the old Maoist condemnation of capitalism after all, for if there is one economic transaction that exemplifies "capitalist decadence", surely this is it – *the importation of plastic turds from thousands of miles away*!

§

2. Some of the beggars in Madrid have taken to putting "Soy español" ("I'm Spanish") on the cardboard signs they use to describe their plight and express their gratitude (in advance...) to the people who are willing to give them something. Their hope is that fellow Spaniards will feel greater solidarity with them, by virtue of their common nationality, than with other, non-Spanish beggars. In short, there now exists *competition among beggars*. Can one imagine a more pathetic instance of capitulation to – or rather, a finer illustration of the triumph of – the logic of "the market"? That the competition is based on national identity is hardly surprising: it was only a matter of time before capitalism, so resourceful when it comes to exploiting national differences to divide ordinary workers and pit them against one another, would find a way to exploit these same divisions even among *those who are unfit to work*.

§

3. The true genius of capitalism is, without a doubt, its *timing*: capitalism carried out the worst of its crimes and atrocities while no one was looking, and long, long before anybody cared.

§

4. Raymond Williams once wrote an essay titled "You're a Marxist, Aren't You?"[1] in which he probed the meaning of this question, or rather the meaning of the "Marxist" label. One matter that he did not consider, however, is the meaning of a related question, namely, Are you *still* a Marxist?, a question often put to thinkers, writers, artists, politicians and so on who at one time professed an adherence to Marxism but whose current ideological orientation is uncertain. (Some of these people hasten to answer the question even when no one asks, as though a pronouncement in this regard were somehow de rigueur.) But what is the person who poses the latter question *really* asking? Clearly the question does *not* mean, say, "Do you still subscribe to the basic tenets of the materialist conception of history?" or "Do you continue to endorse the labor theory of value?" or even "Do you still embrace the view that 'the history of all hitherto existing society is the history of class struggles'?" It obviously cannot mean any of these things, for there is apparently no one proposition that all "Marxists" are supposed to accept, and in any case the figures to whom the question is put typically rejected at least some tenets of classical Marxism even when their identification with Marxist doctrine was most complete. In fact, the question that is *really* being asked is much more narrowly political, namely: *Have you made peace with the system*, or do you still look with favor on left-wing challenges to the status quo? Indeed, it is because this is what is usually being asked that an answer in the negative is so very welcome. (By contrast, who cares whether or not someone remains a "Freudian", or is still a "Nietzschean"?)

§

5. *Militarism as a Way of Life*. Baseball caps, T-shirts, bumper stickers and so on that glorify battleships, army bases, military campaigns, entire wars: where does one find such an unabashed celebration of militarism outside the United States? Or rather, where else do the paraphernalia and accoutrements of militarism assume such *banal* forms? Where else is *pride* in wanton destruction and violence not only

50

tolerated, but even encouraged and praised – indeed, considered *virtuous*? There even exist special issue *license plates* in some areas to indicate that the car's owner is a veteran. The latter will seem unexceptionably "non-militaristic" only if you fail to realize that no such privilege exists for *peace* activists – many of whom are *veterans* of social movements – and others who have resisted militarism, jingoism, imperialist machinations and so on, even if they too have suffered injuries in, as it were, "the line of duty". ... Not surprisingly, when an automobile manufacturer began selling a massive, sinister-looking military vehicle as just another ordinary passenger car, what some Americans found most troubling was its poor *fuel efficiency.*

§

6. "The United States is probably the most open and freest society in the world.... On the other hand, it is also one of the most deeply indoctrinated societies in the world and one of the most depoliticized societies in the world, and one of the societies with the most conformist intelligentsia in the world... So it is not at all paradoxical that in *the most free and open society* you should have *the most sophisticated, well-grafted and effective system of indoctrination and thought control"* (Noam Chomsky).[2]

On the whole this is, of course, quite correct. But is the indoctrination really all that *sophisticated*? Requiring children to recite the "Pledge of Allegiance" while they're still digesting their breakfast, a rendition of the national anthem before every sporting event of any consequence (there's nothing more *politicized* in the U.S. than professional sports), the ubiquity of the American flag, the creation and observance of a day in its honor ("Flag Day") – these are hardly the most sophisticated techniques for instilling patriotism and nationalism; and it is difficult to believe that the American educational system, while not quite so crude in its methods of transmitting propaganda and fostering conformity, is any more refined, at least as far as indoctrination is concerned, than what we find in other advanced nations.

§

7. Just as major challenges to capitalism are crystallizing and gaining momentum, someone invents a medium that is of incomparable efficacy in manipulating perceptions, promoting ideologies, distorting moral sensibilities and sustaining the hegemony of ruling-class values. The religiosity of some contemporary capitalists appears paradoxical only so long as we ignore the invention of television, which was nothing if not a *godsend* to capitalism.

§

8. In one of the most famous passages from his *Autobiography*, John Stuart Mill relates the following episode: "It was in the autumn of 1826. I was in a dull state of nerves... In this frame of mind it occurred to me to put the question directly to myself: 'Suppose that all your objects in life were realised; that all the changes in institutions and opinions which you are looking forward to, could be completely effected at this very instant: would this be a great joy and happiness to you?' And an irrepressible self-consciousness distinctly answered, 'No!' ... All my happiness was to have been found in the continual pursuit of this end. The end had ceased to charm, and how could there ever again be any interest in the means?"[3] What is most remarkable about this passage – though invariably ignored – is Mill's astonishingly *static, ahistorical* sense of his own identity: it never crossed Mill's mind that the profound transformations of society that he envisioned and advocated would, in being realized, leave *him* transformed too. While unlikely to precipitate "humanity's leap from the kingdom of necessity to the kingdom of freedom" (Engels),[4] Mill's reformist program was far-reaching in some respects and potentially quite radical. All the same, he assumes that its implementation would leave people, himself included, more or less as they are – the same desires, hopes, tastes, values, outlook, etc. (suggesting a rather extreme commitment to the conventional economic assumption of "stable preferences"). There is simply no suspicion on Mill's part that even a very partial liberation unleashes repressed potentials and produces momentous changes. As Federico García Lorca once remarked in an interview, "The day that hunger disappears, the world will see a spiritual explosion such as humanity has never known."[5]

§

9. The world-historical "aestheticization of the political" under fascism has blinded us, or at any rate desensitized us, to the *everyday* aestheticization of politics that characterizes most media treatment of political news today. *This* aestheticization of politics begins with the endless analyses of electoral strategies and marketing techniques, the interest in the theatrical aspects of the agon in Washington, the attention devoted to politicians' personalities, the extensive commentary lavished upon inconsequential political gestures, and so on. The main difference with respect to the earlier phenomenon of "aestheticization" is that today we are consciously complicit in our own manipulation, that is, we consciously acquiesce in others' manipulation of us. In fact, we often take an aesthetic interest in the contemplation of our manipulation; we like following the operation: just think of our acritical fascination with media reports on politicians' cynical strategies to win voters or influence public opinion. It is not surprising, then, that for many people "to be well informed" is simply to be duly aware of professional politicians' current strategies of manipulation. (If, as Engels puts it, "the government of persons is replaced by the administration of things"[6] and politics ceases to be a kind of theatrics aimed at consolidating and perpetuating *domination*, the aestheticization of politics will no longer be possible).

§

10. Certain sub-genres of rock music are said to appeal primarily to "alienated youth" and are, it seems, advertised accordingly: once an inspiration for radical social change, alienation now yields a "market demographic"...

§

11. When bourgeois politicians attend funerals *in a political capacity* (for soldiers who have fallen in combat, for the victims of natural disasters or ghastly crimes, etc.), their presence rightly offends us, for they perform a gesture that is *doubly indecent*. It is indecent, in the first place, because the

politicians' presence implies a proximity to their "constituencies" which is, we know, completely spurious. It is additionally indecent because the politicians' own work entails, among other things, meting out violence, which inevitably leads to... more funerals.

§

12. How many of those who grant *a right to privacy* pause to consider *the political economy of privacy*, and hence all that this right really entails with regard to the destitute? Privacy has its material preconditions, too, and for this reason it remains a privilege that many simply do not enjoy. One of the many indignities of being homeless, for example, is an absolute denial of privacy: all of one's activities are inescapably *public* – one eats, sleeps, works, relaxes, urinates, etc. in the public realm. (That this denial or deprivation is not quite so extreme in the case of those who are *merely* dirt poor, without being homeless, does not mean that their privacy is not also severely curtailed, since their condition obliges them to rely on many public goods that the better off can do without.) The right to privacy is a *positive right* if there ever was one.

§

13. American political leaders are, if anything, *arch-relativists* – one set of moral standards for themselves, another for "allies" of the United States, another still for governments on the official enemy list. Why, then, does the alleged "moral relativism" of American youth arouse such indignation and dismay? Should we not, rather, be praising the young, or at least the genuine relativists among them, for the earnestness and thoroughness with which they emulate their natural "role models"?

§

14. Those who deplore some people's readiness to speak bluntly about incomes and earnings fail to appreciate the reactionary effect of an undue "discretion" on these matters. For one thing, to eschew discussing the incomes of different

sectors of society is to forgo the very information that is necessary to mount a serious challenge to the established order and effect real change. For another, such "discretion" reinforces the notion that "one shouldn't think about money," and is thus demeaning to those who willy-nilly *must* spend a good deal of time thinking about it, if they hope to survive. Finally, a reticence on the topic of earnings legitimates – and often betrays an implicit acceptance of – the notion that what one *earns* really does offer a reliable measure of one's true *value*, the reasoning being that, if there were no such relation between monetary worth and, as it were, one's absolute value, there would be no reason for secrecy, since disclosure of this information would not prove offensive to anyone, nor could it be used to justify any social privileges. It is for this last reason that reluctance to disclose one's salary or income epitomizes the psychological triumph of capitalism, confirming as it does a thoroughgoing assimilation of the notion that your *monetary* value is indeed your *real* value.

§

15. An early, official definition (published in *Pravda*, no less) of socialist realism: "Socialist realism ... demands truthfulness from the artist and a historically concrete portrayal of reality in its revolutionary development. Under these conditions, truthfulness and historical concreteness of artistic portrayal ought to be combined with the task of the ideological remaking and education of working people in the spirit of socialism."[7] It is probably seldom noticed that by simply substituting "capitalist" for "socialist" and "capitalism" for "socialism", we can aptly define the practice of *capitalist realism* that informs nearly all the advertising – and much else – produced in capitalist nations today. (Needless to say, we must also qualify the part about "truthfulness", but all the same...)

§

16. "Cultural imperialism" is usually understood, naturally enough, as involving a colonization and appropriation of the cultural space of other nations. However, given that "culture"

55

itself is normally understood in an unduly limited sense, this conventional conception of cultural imperialism in fact proves too narrow. For one thing, it encourages us to ignore that dimension of colonization which consists in *imperial hegemony*, i.e. the process by which the "ruling ideas" of the Empire's ruling class become the "ruling ideas" of the vassal states' dominant classes. Even more important, it leads us to neglect the most obvious correlate of imperialism in the realm of culture: just as classical imperialism consists in the acquisition of territory and natural resources, one of the forms that imperialism takes in the realm of culture involves the plunder of "human capital", as the talented and educated are encouraged (directly, through recruitment and incentives, or indirectly, owing to the absence of other options) to put themselves at the service of the Empire. This particular form of expropriation finds its most dramatic expression in emigration to the metropolis ("the brain drain"), while its crowning achievement is surely to be found in the exodus of *dissidents* (e.g. in pursuit of university posts in the United States), whose departure encourages their political neutralization at the same time as it lends the Empire's self-image a certain objective credibility.

§

17. Charity, as Manuel González Prada once pointed out, "assumes the unequal distribution of wealth, that is to say, injustice. If there is someone who gives alms, it is because there are needy people or men deprived of what is necessary."[8] Indeed, and it is for this very reason that, perverse as it may sound, charity is perhaps *the most emblematic virtue* of capitalism, answering as it does to the system's token failing. For social inequality and an abundance of people lacking "what is necessary" (even when the basic needs of all can be readily satisfied) are the hallmark of capitalism and, on the other hand, charity represents a praiseworthy denial of those impulses – greed, raw self-interest, acquisitiveness and competitive individualism – which, being the mainspring of capitalism, are continuously nurtured and exploited by this "way of life". And this is of course to say nothing of the indispensability of charity in defusing the tensions within

capitalist societies, and in some instances even forestalling their collapse.

§

18. One of the more abject displays of political rectitude, not uncommon in historical works on socialism or the role of intellectuals in twentieth-century politics, consists in denouncing, or at the very least ridiculing, "fellow-travelers" of Stalinism and Soviet Communism generally. For the writers and intellectuals who are given to this sort of exercise invariably ignore the countless hours of fellow-traveling logged by many of their contemporaries, namely those who sympathize with and promote the capitalist parties and governments responsible for so many crimes today. Such neglect is remarkable not only because of the sheer *conspicuousness* of contemporary fellow-traveling as a political phenomenon, but also because the attitude of today's fellow-travelers is far more reprehensible than that of the typical fellow-traveler during, say, the Stalin era. Many of the old communist fellow-travelers persisted in championing indefensible institutions, practices and figures in large part because they had little access to accurate information about the true nature of what they were defending. By contrast, today's fellow-travelers persist in supporting institutions, practices and figures (e.g. American foreign policy, certain international financial institutions, the Leaders of the Free World) whose depravity is perfectly obvious to any informed observer. Indeed, given the superabundance of evidence available, it takes no small effort *not* to see that these things are morally indefensible. If, therefore, one's support for indefensible persons or practices is reprehensible to the extent that one *knows* that they are indefensible, a writer whose sense of political rectitude impels her to condemn fellow-traveling should start by turning her attention to her contemporaries, and if the writer has any integrity, she will have to begin, in all likelihood, by indicting herself.

§

19. How to define *enlightenment* in political culture? Would it not be an *immunity to demagogy?*

§

20. Capitalist society remains unsurpassed in its knack – and propensity – for giving one a material stake in the suffering and demise of others: "For-profit" hospitals, private ambulance companies, the privatization of medical care for the elderly, the arms trade, the celebration of the right to inheritance... All the more reason, then, to wonder about the sanity of those who persist in believing that capitalism is compatible with a truly ecological society, that is, a society devoted to *flourishing* and *life*.

§

21. If left-wing political mobilization proves especially difficult today, it is largely because the exigencies of *disalienation* are more onerous than they were in the past. To be sure, disalienation has always entailed (at least for those who embraced their estrangement) a certain measure of disorientation and disillusion – in a word, *alienation* – for it invariably requires that we dishabituate ourselves to familiar patterns of thought, repudiate certain attitudes, reassess institutions and force ourselves to confront sources of political oppression in practices that we had hitherto regarded as *obviously* non-political. Yet today's media and official mechanisms for political indoctrination tend to foster an even more profound allegiance to the status quo than that which existed in earlier times. This is one reason why we find less receptivity to radical rhetoric and ideas today, and the main reason why the experience of disalienation is even more distressing for us than it was for previous generations.

§

22. The author of *Missing*, a well-known account of US complicity in the assassination of an American citizen in the aftermath of Pinochet's coup in Chile, thought it necessary to append the following "Author's Note" to one edition of his book: "One final note would also appear to be in order. I grew up with an abiding faith in America. It is, in my estimation, the greatest country in the world – not for its wealth or military

might, but because its people have achieved a balance of security, freedom and human rights unmatched in history. The preceding pages have been written, not to cast doubt on this country or the men and women who serve so well in our military and diplomatic corps..."9 One would be hard pressed to find a better illustration of the efficacy of American indoctrination. The writer relates at length an unusually blatant example of the US government's criminal indifference to its own citizens' fate, gives us every reason to infer that such episodes are a natural by-product of American imperial machinations, and rather than urging his readers to question the "abiding faith in America" that blinds Americans to the very evils he has documented, he concludes his book with the True Believer's ritual disclaimer. With intellectuals like this, who needs loyalty oaths?

§

23. It is impossible to imagine a Gramsci, a Luxemburg or any of the other classic Marxists writing for the capitalist press. They were naturally unwilling to accommodate themselves to the confines of such media, and the capitalist press was understandably wary of promoting the activities of committed Marxist revolutionaries. Today, on the other hand, many leftist literati and publicists are quite happy to lend their services to the capitalist press, and the latter regularly open their pages to such writers. While the change in attitude on the part of the capitalist press is not difficult to understand – the Left is no longer perceived as a genuine threat to its interests, and a newspaper's reputation and prestige (and hence *earnings*) can only be enhanced by such displays of tolerance, diversity of opinion and "balance" – what are we to make of this compromise on the part of the left-wing writers themselves? They themselves might well claim, of course, that their writing for the capitalist press in effect subsidizes their work for left-wing causes like alternative media, for they might be unable to devote their time and energy to these causes without the income provided by their "bourgeois" journalism. The only trouble with this line of reasoning is that their contributions to the alternative media frequently consist of the

republication of material that first appeared... in the capitalist press.

§

24. How is it that after a visit to one of the great art museums one does not invariably come away a convert to some progressive social doctrine? For to visit such places is to encounter endless testimony to, and incomparably vivid illustrations of, the sheer *irrationality* and *hideousness* that have stamped so much of human social history, with its monarchs and royalty, its surrender to religious hysteria, its abject embrace of militarism, etc. (By the same token, how can anyone, after a stroll through one of these institutions, fail to appreciate the aspirations of the nineteenth-century positivists?)

§

25. It is a mistake, no doubt, to condemn the soldiers who volunteer to fight in unjust wars (on the instigators' side), just as it is wrong to condemn those who are conscripted to fight. It is not the volunteers' decisions, of course, that cause these wars in the first place, and their enthusiasm and naivety are generally attributable to youthfulness and can be excused on these grounds, at least in part. But what about the volunteers' *parents* (and, for that matter, their older friends and relatives)? What excuse do *they* have for failing to prevent their sons and daughters from taking part in unjust wars? How are parents to justify their failure to resist the familiar blandishments of war propaganda, when they have "seen it all before" and should know better? Indeed, parents who allow their children to become accomplices to what is in fact one of the supreme evils and to endanger their own lives for no good reason are *derelict* parents. Is it really unfair, then, to blame *them* for the steady supply of volunteers ready to fight in unjust wars, and even to hold them responsible, in part, for making these wars possible?

§

26. We demand cheaper goods, knowing full well that lower wages are usually the key to lower prices; members of oppressed groups compete against one another for opportunities and benefits (...and by demanding cheaper goods); radical groups find themselves obliged to use violence in order to combat injustice and oppression: in capitalist societies *moral entrapment* is the order of the day.

§

27. Why does Marxism, the "theory of proletarian self-emancipation", appeal to so many intellectuals? The obvious and most plausible explanation is of course that they find Marxism a more convincing and powerful account of social reality – and in particular the "ever more blatant contradiction between the available resources for liberation and their use for the perpetuation of servitude" (Marcuse)[10] – than rival theories or doctrines. (To paraphrase a remark attributed to Che Guevara, it is not their fault if reality is Marxist.) This is hardly surprising, given that Marx himself incorporated and synthesized the insights of countless previous thinkers, a fact that Lenin himself sought to underscore with his famous explanation of the "three component parts" of Marxism. Furthermore, the outlook and social position of intellectuals typically shields them from some of the influences and pressures that would otherwise predispose them against an acceptance of a Marxist point of view. It is also true, of course, that many of them identify with, and would stand to gain from, the triumph of basic socialist values.

All the same, a good number of right-wing intellectuals, anti-Marxists and non-Marxist "Marxologists" would have us believe that the *real* reason for so many intellectuals' allegiance to Marxism has to do with their need for an ideology that will sanction and promote their own upward mobility, and so derives, in the last analysis, from a self-interested desire for recognition and authority. (This claim is sometimes combined with an additional, even more psychologistic explanation to the effect that intellectuals also turn to Marxism out of hunger for a secular, this-worldly eschatology.) Not surprisingly, those who defend such a view never bother to explain why, assuming they are correct, so *few* intellectuals, relatively speaking, actually end up embracing Marxism. Or why these intellectuals do not turn to other, more readily serviceable ideologies (say, a technocratic creed à la Saint-Simon) in the hope of furthering their corporate interests. Or, for that matter, why the same sort of motivation is not to be imputed to the far greater number of intellectuals who espouse some form or other of liberalism...

§

28. *Anti-Americanism*. The unspeakable habit of applying the same ethical canons to US foreign policy as those which Americans themselves routinely apply to the policies of all other nations in the world.

§

29. Defense of the "work ethic" today generally represents a reactionary attitude, at least to the extent that it involves a commitment to a *capitalist* work ethic. *This* work ethic not only urges us to continue laboring long hours at the very historical juncture in which we ought to be reducing our work time, but also fosters an undiscriminating embrace of work *as such*, rather than reserving its approval for work that is meaningful and inherently satisfying – the only kind of work relevant to a truly enlightened "work ethic".

§

30. From a 1949 article by one J. Salwyn Schapiro: "Any one [sic] who passes from the pages of [John Stuart] Mill to those of Marx becomes acutely aware of a sudden change of intellectual climate. It is the change from tolerant, democratic liberalism to intolerant, authoritarian communism."[11] This opinion – doubtless still widespread today, more than six decades later – confirms the power of *rhetorical civility* to obscure repellent views. For the "intellectual climate" of Mill was in many respects paternalistic, if not positively authoritarian, and undeniably anti-democratic (however tolerant and respectful the tone of Mill's writings). Mill was, after all, a philosopher who approved of a means test for marriage,

believed that those possessed of "mental superiority" should be entitled to more votes than the unlettered, defended capital punishment and regarded "the labouring masses" as an "uncultivated herd".[12] If this is the face of "tolerant, democratic liberalism"...

§

31. "Mass murderers like Stalin, Mao, and Hitler" – variations of this tag are quite common, yet for some inexplicable reason the likes of Richard Nixon, LBJ or Ronald Reagan are systematically excluded from the ranks of "mass murderers". Why is this? After all, they too are mass murderers (or "butchers"), given the criteria implicitly used in applying this epithet to Stalin, Mao, or Hitler. For these figures are called "mass murderers" not on the basis of any killings that they themselves may have personally carried out, but because of the deadly actions that they ordered, or the lethal measures that they implemented or encouraged. But, of course, Lyndon B. Johnson, Richard Nixon and Ronald Reagan also enforced policies that led to massive numbers of deaths. Perhaps, then, it is a question of absolute numbers. But apart from the fact that scale would seem to be irrelevant after a certain threshold – does anyone really believe that the person who causes a million deaths is a mass murderer, while the one who causes "merely" a hundred thousand is not? – we should bear in mind that the Vietnam War alone took a few million lives. Indeed, it is beyond dispute that Nixon and LBJ were jointly responsible for more deaths than, say, Pol Pot. Perhaps what is really decisive is the rulers' intentions. Yet even the most bloodthirsty dictators often profess the noblest of aims – justice, freedom, human emancipation, and the like. Or perhaps it is rather the case that most people neglect to include figures like Reagan and Nixon within the set of "mass murderers" for the simple reason that American presidents were elected politicians acting in the name of "democratic" governments, while this is not true of, say, Stalin and Mao. But this is plainly irrelevant when assessing the appropriateness of the "mass murderer" label, given that the deaths in question, as far as the American presidents are concerned, *occurred in other countries*, where the decisions of American

politicians are wholly devoid of political legitimacy, and hence enjoy no more democratic legitimacy than decisions made by dictators. So, then, why *are* American presidents never called "mass murderers"? Why is *their* responsibility never acknowledged?

§

32. In *What is to Be Done?* Lenin insists that "class political consciousness can be brought to the workers *only from without,* that is, only from outside the economic struggle, from outside the sphere of relations between workers and employers."[13] Lenin was probably mistaken at the time he wrote these words, more than a century ago, but his thesis seems true enough today. After all, workers enter "the sphere of relations between workers and employers" with a good deal more formal education than they did in Lenin's era, and if they are *better educated,* they will inevitably be *better indoctrinated* too.

§

33. *Blame America First.* Why does this principle arouse such hostility? Is it not in fact a perfectly sensible heuristic – indeed, the obvious methodological rule of thumb for anyone who knows the first thing about world history since 1945?

§

34. *The opium of the people.* Many who are unfamiliar with the context of this famous passage erroneously assume that Marx is claiming (à la Meslier) that the dominant classes deliberately administer the narcotic of religious superstition to the masses, in the hope of keeping them docile and contented. Of course, *were* this Marx's point, the analysis would be perfectly applicable as a description of how most "conservative" intellectuals instrumentalize religion today, endlessly proclaiming the value, importance and indispensability of religion, all the while maintaining their own (pious) irreligiosity.

As for the "opium of the people": is it not remarkable that religious sects prove so obliging in providing *corroboration* for Marx's interpretation of religion, as they shamelessly proselytize among the downtrodden, marginalized, disadvantaged and oppressed?

§

35. We dread appearing *dated*, in part because we associate "datedness" with aging and *death*, which, along with the countless other indignities it visits upon us, *dates us definitively*. Consumer capitalism shrewdly exploits this fear of becoming dated, plying us with goods (clothing, furnishings, etc.) that ensure a certain measure of *existential* currency, while continually threatening to date us far more efficiently and ruthlessly than any other socio-economic arrangement, thanks to its incessant delivery of new products and new styles. To embrace consumerism is, for this reason, to consent to the exploitation of one's own vulnerability – indeed, to revel in it.

§

36. For all the braying and clucking on the part of right-wing publicists and intellectuals, the "capitalist class" has no quarrel with the presence of Marxists in the academy. For one thing, the academy tends to neutralize all radicals, dissidents and subversives, so it can be trusted to depoliticize most Marxist intellectuals too. For another, such "tolerance" makes the system *look good* – indeed, it seems to embody and hence confirm capitalist society's self-image (the "open society"). Finally, and not least of all, academic Marxists often produce some very interesting work, which, besides enriching intellectual culture as a whole, will be valued and appreciated even by conservatives.

§

37. One scarcely acknowledged consequence of American imperialism is a certain *parochialization* of the world's political culture. The United States possesses an empire, and hence

American political culture is inevitably an object of universal concern: people around the world are well informed about, and often take considerable interest in, the major developments in American politics. As a result of this interest and the scope of "cultural imperialism" (American pundits' views are reprinted in newspapers on every continent), the political analyses produced by American commentators automatically assume the status of *universal* culture, no matter how provincial the views of the commentators themselves and no matter how insignificant the topics to which they devote their attention. Imperialism thus succeeds in impoverishing the political culture of subject nations, as though it were not content to impoverish every other dimension of their cultures.

§

38. Even many on the Left fail to recognize the extent to which the prestige of *veterans* in American society promotes an insidious militarism and is therefore detrimental to progressive causes. (The situation is very different in most other democracies, in that the category of *veteran* seems to play no role whatsoever in their political culture.) While it is true that many veterans once "put their lives on the line", it is equally true that many *did not*, that is, that many who served in the armed forces never experienced combat or warfare at first hand. At the same time, many ordinary people who have fought against militarism, jingoism, unjust wars and the like have also "put their lives on the line" – by engaging in certain acts of civil disobedience, by exposing themselves to the "crowd control" measures used to suppress controversial demonstrations, by daring to exercise certain rights to dissent and by condemning and opposing the activities of violent, reactionary organizations – quite apart from the personal sacrifices, in terms of time and energy, that they must make, and the vilification that they often have to endure. One might argue, of course, that military service always potentially exposes one to some risk of personal injury, whereas the possibility of such danger is a much more contingent matter in the case of political activism, but this contrast is clearly bogus when it is a question of resolute "anti-system" activism. By accepting the greater prestige accorded to military service,

66

then, Leftists in effect lend their support to the view that this form of commitment is inherently more worthy, more honorable and more admirable than, say, anti-militarist activism, and so not only do a disservice to those engaged in the latter, but actually help to foster the very militarist ethos that they claim to condemn. (It is because of the sheer pervasiveness of this ethos that an embrace of American militarism is typically one of the first concessions that the American "ex-Leftist" makes in his bid for inclusion and respectability.)

It is also worth recalling in this connection that in the United States the phrase "to serve one's country" is almost invariably associated with military service. No matter that one may be doing more to benefit one's country – be *serving its interests* more effectively – by engaging in, say, anti-militarist activities, or that by "serving humanity" we might at one and the same time be "serving our country". In any event, the more fundamental point, of course, is that there is nothing *intrinsically* virtuous about military service; it is, rather, a morally neutral activity, its value depending on the goals and purposes for which one fights. Likewise, if you do not believe that there is anything virtuous, admirable or commendable about patriotism *as such*, what reason is there for you to believe that military service on behalf of the nation is *necessarily* virtuous, admirable or commendable?

Reverence for military distinction may be our most shameful atavism.

§

39. As one indication of the degree of indoctrination among many intellectuals – even the "critical" and "progressive" ones – consider the following: the very intellectuals who will spare no trouble to track down and read obscure or esoteric books, papers, documents and other sources of information in their desire to "have all the facts" or "get as complete a picture as possible" when it is a matter of their scholarly interests, typically rely on the commercial media for most of their news and tend to grant the veracity of the information available in these media. In other words, the critical attitude that they have cultivated as scholars, the attitude that determines and

sustains the quality of their work by preventing them from accepting anything at face value, the discipline that compels them to *question* relentlessly – this attitude is more or less completely suspended when they occupy themselves with the content of the "news". How are we to explain this contrast – the tremendous disparity between the exigencies of their scholarly conscience and their credulity vis-à-vis the news – if not by the effect of indoctrination? How else to explain the fact that what is in principle the most suspect, most questionable, least credible information happens to be the very information whose veracity, objectivity and credibility they are least likely to challenge? How else to explain that the very people who are so keen in spotting ideological distortion, so adept at perceiving the operation of propaganda, when it occurs *in other places...*

§

40. Mao famously proclaimed that "Political power grows out of the barrel of a gun."[14] If contemporary imperialism has taught us anything, it is that "moral authority", too, *grows out of the barrel of a gun.*

§

41. Politicians and the press in the "democratic" nations sometimes scoff at those former soldiers and revolutionaries who, after becoming *political* leaders, continue to wear military garb. (Needless to say, if the ex-soldier happens to be a faithful servant of the Empire, his dress is a matter of respectful indifference.) But whatever else we may say against the preference for military accoutrements, we ought at least to recognize that the leaders who favor this sort of dress exhibit a commitment to *transparency* that is quite foreign to politicians in the "democratic" nations. For the business of the state is in large part the administration of violence (recall Weber's celebrated characterization of the state), and the soldier in uniform represents nothing if not the administration of "legitimate" violence.

§

42. The first comprehensive translations of Gramsci's writings to be published in the United States appeared in a series that would eventually comprise four large volumes: *Selections from the Prison Notebooks*, two tomes of *Selections from Prison Writings*, and *Selections from Cultural Writings*. The first three volumes, all issued between 1971 and 1978, were published by International Publishers, the publishing arm of the Communist Party of the United States; the final volume, the *Cultural Writings*, was published in 1985 by a university press – *Harvard* University Press, no less. As symbolic testimony to the fate of Marxist theory and Marxist political culture more generally, this publishing history *speaks volumes*.

§

43. It is hard to believe that so many on the Left accept the idea that a university ought to be something of an inviolable sanctum, this being, well, a thoroughly *bourgeois* notion. (It is partly because of this belief that police incursions into universities arouse such indignation, even when these actions do not prove nearly as violent as the less spectacular but far more frequent police assaults on poor neighborhoods.) Why should the university be regarded as somehow detached from the surrounding community, completely insulated from the forces that affect the rest of society, essentially uninvolved in – and untouched by – the processes that stamp everything else? And what about the socio-economic background of most of those who inhabit the sanctum?

Oddly enough, this view is probably more common in Europe than in the United States, where it proves more defensible. After all, many American colleges and universities consist of self-contained, more or less self-sufficient communities with only a tenuous connection to the surrounding city or town. This relative independence from the surrounding community certainly offers a better justification for claims of autonomy and inviolability than the structure of universities on the European model. In reality, of course, American universities enjoy even less autonomy than their European counterparts, while the main effect of their relative independence from neighboring populations seems to be the depoliticization of student life.

§

44. In one of his books, Carlos Franqui, an uncommonly self-aggrandizing Cuban exile, recounts (approvingly) how Octavio Paz once rebuked Gabriel García Márquez for his friendship with Fidel Castro and even accused García Márquez of having "sullied [him]self with the blood of [Castro's] crimes"[15] for having shaken hands with Fidel at a luncheon. Both Paz and Franqui plainly seem to have forgotten the most elemental truth of world politics, namely, that *all politicians of any consequence have dirty hands*. Indeed, in comparison with the hands of, say, any American President from the last half century, with their myriad layers of filth, Fidel Castro's hands appear practically spotless.

§

45. One conservative effect of newspapers: in the course of working our way through a "quality" newspaper we experience the illusion of having learned a good deal, augmented our store of knowledge and enriched our understanding of the world. As a result, we tend to think that we do not need to read and learn much more about the world, and we therefore see no need to have more time available for the activities of reading, learning, thinking, and so on. Hence no demands are made for more *free* time – e.g. for a shorter workweek – at least not on these grounds. Society as presently organized seems to afford us sufficient time for a rich, full intellectual life (the papers' book reviews and Sunday supplements are meant to satisfy even the most demanding and inquisitive of readers). The impetus for some of the most radical of potential political demands is thus effectively neutralized.

§

46. *It is always acceptable to use morally neutral ("non-evaluative") language in referring to the crimes of American imperialism.* This is one of the basic, tacit precepts of

70

"mainstream" political culture in the United States and, alas, much of the rest of the world. Hence the unexceptional character of an essay, published in a leading American literary magazine, in which the author uses the adjective "stupid" to characterize US sponsorship of the 1954 coup in Guatemala,[16] an action that prompted a civil war, led to over one hundred thousand civilian deaths and gave rise to a system of repression of almost unimaginable ferocity. Another writer concludes a book review in a respected journal with these words: "In the end, whatever one thinks of the U.S. invasion [of Panama]...,"[17] the implication being that decent people could reasonably approve of a military operation that led to the slaughter of, at the very least, several hundred harmless civilians in order to capture one petty criminal. As Noam Chomsky observed more than four decades ago in considering the language in which the US political class debated the war in Vietnam, the appropriate term for this sort of perspective and analysis is *moral degeneration.*[18] Of course, it goes without saying that these same writers would never be satisfied with the word "stupid" to describe, say, the Soviet invasion of Czechoslovakia, or that they would not hesitate to denounce any essay on World War II that included the phrase, "Whatever one thinks of the Japanese attack on Pearl Harbor..."

§

47. It is sometimes noted that socialism was attempted in circumstances in which failure was foreordained (Russia) and never given a chance in the very milieu where it was most likely to succeed (Western Europe). This is, to be sure, part of the tragedy of Marxist socialism. But it would perhaps be even more instructive to say that the real tragedy of Marxist socialism is that *economically, it came too soon* and *politically, it came too late.* Too soon economically: if communists had had computers at their disposal from the very first, many of the production and distribution problems (that is, the notorious difficulties attending the dissemination of information) would have proven tractable, if not wholly resolvable. Too late politically: despite their own scandalously undemocratic origins and long history of indifference to the very rights which they claim to represent today, the liberal capitalist demo-

71

cracies have succeeded in delegitimizing the very measures (expropriations, challenges to the prerogatives and liberties of the over-privileged and in general those "despotic inroads on the rights of property, and on the conditions of bourgeois production"[19] mentioned in the *Communist Manifesto*) that are indispensable in laying the foundations for a truly socialist society.

§

48. In Madrid's Ermita de San Antonio de la Florida church one can view various frescos painted by Goya. When Goya created these works, the visitor learns from a text accompanying the exhibit, he "had triumphed as a court painter and was recovering from a serious illness which had left him deaf, as a result of which his view of the world tended to a more critical attitude." Goya's personal evolution thus provides a noteworthy confirmation of the idea that it is exposure to indoctrination, rationalizations and propaganda. that habituates us to the unacceptable. When our exposure to such messages declines – through deafness, for example – our tolerance of the unacceptable declines as well.

§

49. When a professional boxer bit off parts of his opponent's ears during a 1997 heavyweight championship match, many boxing fans – and, for that matter, many with no interest in the sport – voiced their consternation and disgust. Among those who had watched the fight was the President of the United States, Bill Clinton, who was quoted as saying that he was "horrified" by the incident.[20] Incredibly, no one appreciated the irony in the President's words, which is itself testimony to the thoroughgoing perversion of our moral sensibility. For are we not supposed to be less severe in judging those acts of violence committed when the perpetrator is not "in his right mind" (owing to hysteria, rage, desperation, jealousy, etc.), reserving our harshest condemnation and punishment for acts of violence that are the product of dispassionate premeditation? If this is correct, then however gruesome and disturbing the boxer's action – committed, let us not forget, while he was

subject to an extreme degree of physical and psychological stress – we should find it far less "horrifying" than, say, Clinton's own decision to bomb Iraq four years earlier, a decision which, calmly taken in a setting of physical security and material comfort, led to the death of a major Iraqi artist and her husband, and partially blinded their daughter. But, of course, the action ordered by Clinton is never described as "horrifying", and neither are the countless other Presidential directives that have entailed prodigious doses of violence, even when the operations inevitably killed innocents. Likewise, while the boxer issued a public apology shortly after biting his opponent's ears, Clinton has never apologized to the numerous victims or relatives of victims of the lethal measures that he personally authorized. Nor will he ever be expected to do so, unless we finally come to realize that there is far less to censure in the conduct of ear-chomping boxers than in the decisions of those who, living privileged lives in comfort and safety, order brutal assaults on vulnerable populations in distant lands.

§

50. *The essential schizophrenia of capitalist culture.* We are told, time and again, that self-interest is, deep down, the only source of motivation for human beings and, indeed, that the genius of capitalism lies in its capacity to exploit this self-interest for the benefit of all: witness the endless variations on the theme of "private vices, public benefits", or the Right's fondness for citing Adam Smith's famous remark: "It is not from the benevolence of the butcher, the brewer or the baker that we expect our dinner, but from their regard to their own interest. We address ourselves not to their humanity but to their self-love, and never talk to them of our own necessities but of their advantages."[21] At the very same time, we face a deluge of advertisements assuring us that faceless corporations genuinely care about our personal welfare, or that giant companies want to do everything within their power to help us prosper, or that a business's primary motivation for selling us its products or providing its services arises from a concern with our individual happiness, etc., etc.

51. Uncle Sam has always entertained a most idiosyncratic conception of freedom and democracy, but in the old days he at least had the courage of his convictions, acting on this conception without the slightest reserve. It is enough to recall the content of the Platt Amendment, which the United States forced Cuba to include in the Cuban Constitution of 1901. Article III of the Amendment, for example, provides that "the Government of Cuba consents that the United States may exercise the right to intervene for the preservation of Cuban independence, the maintenance of a government adequate for the protection of life, property, and individual liberty, and for discharging the obligations with respect to Cuba imposed by the Treaty of Paris on the United States, now to be assumed and undertaken by the government of Cuba." With this Amendment, then, the US openly proclaimed its right *to intervene in another nation's affairs in order to preserve that nation's independence.* Yet, intriguing as this notion of independence-through-subjugation is, what is truly remarkable about the Article, and the Amendment as a whole, is the near absence of any guile or duplicity. Indeed, we could hardly hope for a more transparent statement of the US's true commitment to freedom and democracy abroad.

§

52. *Bereft of the Radical Muse.* The main problem with so many notable "ex-Marxist" philosophers, thinkers, writers and the like is that after repudiating their former theoretical adherence to Marxism they cease to be... *interesting.* This is not, of course, because their espousal of Marxist theory or Marxist views was what made them interesting, but rather because the repudiation of a Marxist outlook is, as often as not, a reflection or result of the repudiation of a vital critical impulse, one that had been shaped and guided by their commitment to Marxism, the great *counter-heuristic* of our time. Once this impulse is exhausted, once these figures cease thinking against the status quo, there is no need for them to exercise their former resourcefulness, their work assumes more a conventional hue and so tends to become *dull.*

What does it mean to speak of Marxism as a counter-heuristic, or rather *the* great anti-capitalist counter-heuristic of the twentieth century (which is when Marxism as a form of critique truly came into its own and won adherents by the millions)? In Paul A. Baran's words, "Marxism is nothing if not a powerful magnifying glass under which the irrationality of the capitalist system protrudes in all of its monstrous forms." And if this magnifying glass remains indispensable, it is because "the mentality of the dominant class has become undisputedly the dominant mentality, and ... the systematically cultivated attitude of taking capitalism for granted, of considering it to be the obvious, the natural order of things, has become not merely the attitude of the bourgeoisie but the attitude of broad popular masses as well."[22]

§

53. Anyone who doubts the value of ideological hegemony would do well to consider the fate of "human rights" in the era of neo-imperialism. Mention of "human rights violations" typically conjures up images of political prisoners or persecuted religious minorities and not, say, civilian casualties of imperialist aggression. Which is to say, the jailing of a dissident journalist and the repression of religious movements are regarded as more severe human rights violations than the *deaths of non-combatants* at the hands of invading armies. This distortion in our estimation of the relative gravity of these evils is one of imperialism's signal achievements: the imperialist – hence *war-making* – nations' worst crimes do not register as human rights violations, since such things simply do not occur in war (save for the occasional "crimes against humanity" and kindred atrocities, which in any case are *never* committed by the imperialist powers themselves), while far less extreme human rights abuses are considered absolute infamies.

§

54. American *nationalism* is almost invariably characterized as *patriotism*, both within the United States and in the rest of the world. This misperception, or rather mis-identification, is

75

far more significant than most realize, if only because it proves such a boon to US imperialism. By and large nationalism gets a bad press, and *extreme* nationalism is almost universally condemned as beyond the pale. Patriotism, on the other hand, is seldom considered objectionable in itself; on the contrary, it is, as often as not, thought to be praiseworthy. While "nationalism" conjures up images of tribalism, racism, systematic discrimination and "ethnic cleansing", patriotism is usually associated with loyalty, civic responsibility, even solidarity. Thus, if the support for American military actions – which are themselves systematically mislabeled as *defensive* operations – is thought to derive from patriotism rather than nationalism, this support will automatically enjoy at the very least a modicum of legitimacy. And if the support seems legitimate, i.e. seems *justified*, the action will likewise seem legitimate, likewise seem justified (no matter that this is to invert the correct form of reasoning, namely, "It's justified, *therefore* I support it.")

§

55. "Does the consecration of Sunday confess the desecration of the entire week?" asked Emerson long ago.[23] We can only wonder how the Sage of Concord would have viewed the meaning, or rather purpose, of this consecration under late capitalism, when the promise of Sunday is that it offers an alibi for the (momentary) rejection of market rationality and the (momentary) sovereignty of non-market values. Or, for that matter, how he would have viewed the creeping desecration of even this day of the week, as it succumbs to *capitalist* secularization...

§

56. *Khomeini in Paris.* One of the splendid ironies of late twentieth-century politics occurred when the Ayatollah Khomeini was forced to take up residence in Paris during the final months of his exile from Iran. Just imagine: a champion of counter-Enlightenment reaction ends up living in the City of Light! An arch-prude makes his home amidst a people whose culture is the very embodiment of urbane sensuality! Of

course, some might think that the real irony is that this Parisian sojourn did nothing to compromise or taint Khomeini in the eyes of the faithful; after all, he had willingly removed to godless Paris. But to believe this is to forget that for the likes of a Khomeini, living in Paris was tantamount to an act of penance, or at best a kind of desert exile.

§

57. History is indeed "written by the victors", but they enjoy a good deal of assistance from the media and obliging "political analysts". For example, it was not long ago that *El País* matter-of-factly informed its readers that the first free elections in the history of Nicaragua had taken place in *1990*. Is this sort of distortion really any different, at bottom, from the crude falsification of photographs at the hands of Stalin's lackeys? If there is any difference, it is surely one of degree and not kind, a picture being worth a thousand words.

§

58. Why has Marxism in the United States been so susceptible to academic neutralization? Why, that is, have so many American Marxists – and still more semi-Marxist radicals – ended up in universities (as has even been the case with a number of former *Weathermen*)? In addition to the obvious privileges attaching to an academic career – which at good universities can approximate the ideal of unalienated labor – and the undeniable appeal of institutions that respect the aims of *theory*, one important factor has been that American universities seem less *bourgeois* than those of Europe. This is partly because they have historically been somewhat less "classist" and more democratic than their Old World counterparts, and partly because they seem to represent a haven for, or even the embodiment of, *anti-bourgeois* values. The irony is that the mass incorporation of radicals into the academy has coincided with an attenuation of both of these characteristics: the assault on the welfare state is producing a de-democratization of the universities (there is, for example, less money available for needier students), while at the same time the business view of the world and the values of "the

market" now permeate university life, and in many academic institutions already enjoy a kind of unchallenged sovereignty.

§

59. *To die for one's country.* It seems to be almost universally assumed that *any* soldier who dies in battle has *died for his country* (that is, any soldier in a national army or representing a recognized government). But this belief actually proves quite groundless, even if we grant that there do exist genuine "national interests" and that this expression does not always represent an exercise in obfuscation, an attempt to conceal what are in fact particular, typically economic, interests. If "dying for one's country" means anything (and may rightly be judged a supremely virtuous act), it can only mean death *in defense of* one's country, or rather death in *legitimate* defense of its *legitimate* vital interests. Governments, however, often pursue objectives that are detrimental to the true national interest, which is one of the reasons for the existence of *dissent,* or adopt policies that are grossly immoral and hence *unworthy of anyone's country.* If a particular government's policies are grossly immoral or fundamentally at odds with a country's true national interests, what reason is there to say that those who must sacrifice their lives in defense of such policies "die for their country"? Or do we really think that all those German soldiers who fought – often involuntarily, to be sure – and died for Hitler's government "gave their lives for their country"? Or that in civil wars *all* of the soldiers who are killed die for their country, even if one side is plainly in the wrong? Or that it is enough to have the *conviction* that one is dying for one's country?

What percentage, then, of those who have lost their lives in battle really have "died for their country"? The actual percentage is no doubt negligible, despite all the militarist cant to the contrary. Indeed, have more than a handful of American soldiers truly died *for their country* since the end of World War II?

§

60. A writer who sympathized with a far-right political movement during the 1930s was, according to a book that discusses this aspect of his life, "seduced by totalitarianism". Assuming that such a description is fitting, one wonders why it is never said that those figures – intellectuals, writers, academics and so on – who, say, supported the Vietnam War (and often continue to justify it to this day) were "seduced by genocidal imperialism". Or, for that matter, why is it never said that Churchill, who once pronounced himself "strongly in favour of using poisoned gases against uncivilised tribes,"[24] allowed himself to be "seduced by racist exterminationism". Then again, perhaps there is no real mystery here. Use of a word like "seduced" to describe a bad choice made by *someone else* makes the choice appear doubly reprehensible: not only was it a bad choice, but it was also an *irrational* choice. Of course, one might just as well point to the temporary irrationality of those who were "seduced" by totalitarianism (as opposed to dispassionately embracing it) as a circumstance that mitigates their responsibility for such a disastrous choice, whereas those whose defense of murderous policies flows from their considered judgments would seem to have no excuse at all for *their* atrocious decisions. But since this kind of reasoning requires a certain measure of impartiality...

§

61. *The wonders of indoctrination.* One of the countless injustices or enormities committed by the US government comes to light and is investigated, and subsequently some individual, group or institution receives a mild sanction: *voilà – the system works!* It's self-correcting, and should make us proud! It is above all the crudeness of the fallacy underlying this sort of thinking that reveals the depth and efficiency of indoctrination in the United States: one infers from the fact that we become aware of *some* misdeeds, which are then investigated, the conclusion that we know about *all* of the misdeeds for which the government is responsible. (What would our opinion be of any other purportedly "self-correcting" device or institution that detected few of its own errors and was incapable of preventing their recurrence?)

63. Leftists were right to criticize the major Communist parties (in particular the old Moscow-aligned parties in the West) for many things, but the *bourgeois* character of these parties was not one of them. Indeed, those who bemoaned the bourgeois character of the major CPs betrayed a surprising socio-political obtuseness. If the CPs made many concessions to *bourgeois* propriety, it was precisely because they sought to be *workers'* parties, and the great majority of workers had themselves embraced and internalized core bourgeois values and aspirations. In other words, these parties were right to assume what was in many respects a bourgeois sensibility insofar as this was the sensibility of most workers themselves. As Lenin reminds us, "We can (and must) begin to build socialism, not with abstract human material, or with human material specially prepared by us, but with the human material bequeathed to us by capitalism."[25] It is also worth remembering in this regard that many of Marx's own values and tastes were essentially *bourgeois* values and tastes. Indeed, the old CPs could rightfully claim that at least their conservative "moral sensibility" was authentically "Marxian", in that it was quite consistent with, and thus a faithful continuation of, Marx's own moral traditionalism.

64. One of the Right's contemporary strategies aims at convincing Leftists that they must categorically renounce any political option that departs ever so slightly from an exclusively peaceful, more or less intra-institutional pursuit of their political objectives. The arguments that the Right presents for rejecting anything smacking of "armed struggle" are, variously, that political violence cannot, or can no longer, be justified (democracy has supposedly been consolidated in those countries in which insurrection may once have seemed legitimate); that it is inhumane; that it is futile; that it leads to "totalitarianism" and that it is counterproductive. Yet why should Leftists forswear *any* option merely in order to ingratiate themselves with the *Right*? And how can they be expected to abjure what is effectively a right to self-defense?

Above all, where is the Right's sense of *reciprocity*, or rather, *noblesse oblige*? Should it not likewise renounce all recourse to counter-revolutionary violence, reduce the size of its armies and curtail the reach of its police?

§

65. A.'s last human contact before passing away happened to be with the neighbors' son, who, less than an hour before the old man's death, appeared on his doorstep, hoping to fob something off on him as part of a "fundraiser". This particular mode of farewell is, alas, probably not uncommon nowadays: "Raising funds" (e.g. for investment) has been essential to the operation of capitalism from the very start, but in recent years the non-commercial "fundraiser" has also become an important rite in American society, as every sort of organization, society, club and association now relies on this practice to ensure its own continued existence. Though hardly acknowledged, the ubiquity of fundraisers today represents a twofold triumph for the "spirit of capitalism". First, and most obviously, the phenomenon reflects an *economic* triumph: fundraisers are now used in many cases to provide the wherewithal for activities and services that were once provided by the state but whose costs must now be borne by the private institutions of "civil society". Second, fundraisers testify to a *psychological* triumph: to the extent that fundraisers (such as bake sales, auctions, flea markets and concerts) involve *receiving* something in exchange for one's "charitable contribution", they foster the expectation that our charity *entitles* us to something. Which is to say, fundraisers offer us yet another instance in which the bourgeoisie "has drowned the most heavenly ecstasies of religious fervour, of chivalrous enthusiasm, of philistine sentimentalism, in the icy water of egotistical calculation" (*Communist Manifesto*).[26]

§

66. *Think for yourself – within reason.* Two large decals were on display on the truck's rear window. One decal urged us all to "question authority"; the other featured a big, bright American flag.

81

§

67. In the introduction to an interview with Daniel Bell, Peter Beilharz writes, "As [Bell] likes to say, his views are conservative in culture, liberal in politics, socialist in economics." Beilharz then adds: "The mix is as eminently sensible as it is fascinating."[27] In fact, "the mix", i.e. Bell's self-definition, is eminently *absurd*, as the interviewer, the editor of a journal heavily influenced by Marxist social theory, ought to have realized. How can one consistently be a "liberal in politics" (in any conventional sense) and a "socialist in economics" (in any substantive sense), when even minimally socialist measures require the curtailing or abrogation of certain rights – property rights, investment rights, claims to inheritance, etc. – essential to political liberalism? (*Every* social arrangement restricts or denies *some* "rights" in order to establish or protect *other* "rights".) And does anyone really believe that a genuinely socialist economy would be compatible with, or rather would leave unmodified, a society's existing (i.e. pre-socialist) cultural life? How, for example, could the class-distorted thought-patterns and perceptions that shape cultural life today be compatible with the fundamental social equality that socialism both requires and creates? On the other hand, how could one believe that the enormous expansion of opportunities for people created by a truly socialist economy – a powerful stimulus to the emergence of new ideas, initiatives and *demands* – will leave cultural life more or less unchanged?

The basic problem is that Bell's self-definition (echoed by several other thinkers, such as Leszek Kolakowski, who characterized himself in more or less identical terms) assumes, erroneously, that we can neatly compartmentalize politics, economics and culture, as though these spheres were not, practically speaking, thoroughly intertwined. Yet one need hardly embrace some exotic notion of "totality" to believe that these spheres are inseparably interconnected. In any case, Bell and the others could of course qualify the liberal-conservative-socialist label, but if thoroughgoing qualification is necessary, as it surely is, why bother using the label at all?

§

68. A decline in political news during the summer vacation period, with its attendant "depoliticization" of radio and television programming, fosters the notion that politics, too, is a kind of business activity, quite foreign to life's essential matters and one from which we rightly take a yearly vacation (as is the case with other kinds of business). One result is that people are encouraged to abstain from political activity and engagement, and reduce their interest in politics as such, at the very time when they are freest – i.e. have the most *time* – to think about the *res publica* and to assert themselves politically. In short, we are discouraged from thinking and acting politically during the very period in which we are, in one sense, in the best position to... think and act politically. This is no small victory for those who gain from the wholesale institutionalization of civic activity and the political neutralization of the public.

§

69. Thomas Paine argued that America's – that is, the nascent United States' – pristine quality made it a uniquely suitable milieu for the creation of a new, enlightened, truly just society: "So deeply rooted were all the governments of the old world, and so effectually had the tyranny and the antiquity of habit established itself over the mind, that no beginning could be made in Asia, Africa, or Europe, to reform the political condition of man... As America was the only spot in the political world, where the principles of universal reformation could begin, so also was it the best in the natural world."[28] What Paine failed to foresee was the extent to which this freedom from all of the blights that had shaped history in Europe and elsewhere – the fact that, as Rodó put it, paraphrasing Baudelaire, Americans were born "with the *innate experience* of freedom"[29] – was also a *disadvantage*, an *obstacle*, in that a deep historical memory of oppression, pain, suffering and struggle – a prime source of inspiration for radical political action – would also be lacking, left behind, as it were, in the immigrants' homelands.

To put the point a bit differently, we could say that the greatest impediment to processes of *democratization* – not to mention socialism – in the US may well be, paradoxically,

Americans' familiarity with "democracy". The United States, unlike, for example, the nations of Europe, came into being as a democracy of sorts. Americans are consequently less apt to view democracy as a result of historical processes – namely, the struggles for a democratization of society. In short, American democracy is not seen as the embodiment of hard-won gains; rather, one regards it as a fait accompli, and one which occurred, neatly and effortlessly, when the nation achieved its independence ("the Founding Fathers designed the United States as a democracy"). This mindset produces a general complacency, while also discouraging serious debate of proposals for substantive democratization: if the consolidation of "democracy" is presupposed, anyone who insists on the need to "democratize" society will inevitably sound like something of a crank. In any case, given that this experience of "democracy" tends to inhibit attempts at a truly thoroughgoing democratization of society, it is hardly surprising that a de Tocqueville would reckon it an *advantage*. "The great advantage of the Americans," he remarked, "is that they have come to democracy without having to endure democratic revolutions; and that they are born equal, instead of becoming so."[30]

§

70. Lest there be any doubts about the recent victory of capitalism and the complete *neutralization* – for the moment – of communism: El Corte Inglés, Spain's largest department-store chain and icon of Spanish entrepreneurial achievement, stocks a reasonable supply of communist and left-wing literature (modern editions of the *Manifesto*, sympathetic expositions of, and commentaries on, Marxist views or figures, contemporary statements of communist ideas, etc.) in some of its bookstores. In other words, not only is it the case that big capital no longer perceives communist ideas as the least bit *threatening*; it even thinks that it can make a profit off them.

§

71. To be sure, television *depoliticizes*, as is often pointed out, to the extent that it succeeds in disseminating ruling

class ideology with an unmatched efficiency and insidious-ness, while at the same time atomizing or fragmenting the public. Yet television also induces depoliticization, or in any case acceptance of the status quo, insofar as it functions as a drug of sorts for countless viewers – soothing, relaxing and pacifying them. For many people, the images that are *sanctioned* by television (because they are presented in a favorable light, or because they form part of the regular – i.e. antecedently endorsed – programming) are associated with reassuring feelings, and are, accordingly, reckoned good, respectable, normal and proper. By the same token, the words, gestures and actions that seem incompatible with the sanctioned images, along with the people who challenge those images, are usually perceived as uncongenial, if not hostile, abnormal and *dangerous*. (As such considerations remind us, we should speak of *asthetico-cultural hegemony*, rather than "cultural imperialism", in trying to explain the *domination* that is maintained and reinforced through the "media".)

§

72. *The incongruity of being a "conservative" in the United States.* Here is a country (and a relatively *young* one at that) in which nothing is, or can be, "conserved" in that the dynamics of American capitalism, and perhaps the American Way of Life generally, are quite inimical to the conservation of anything in the way of traditions, customs, social conventions, lifestyles, and so on. Indeed, if ever there were an example of the "constant revolutionising of production, uninterrupted disturbance of all social conditions, [and] everlasting uncertainty and agitation [which] distinguish the bourgeois epoch from all earlier ones," if ever there were a society in which "all fixed, fast-frozen relations, with their train of ancient and venerable prejudices and opinions, are swept away, [and] all new-formed ones become antiquated before they can ossify,"[31] surely it is the contemporary United States. In such conditions as these, what is left for the conservative to affirm, uphold, or commemorate? (Perhaps these circum-stances explain in part – that is, along with the context of an uncommonly impoverished political culture – why so many Americans were prepared to accept Ronald Reagan's claim to

85

be *both* a conservative and a revolutionary, as though the very notion of revolution were not anathema to all genuine conservatives.)

Neil Postman once observed that "the United States is the most radical society in the world. It is in the process of conducting a vast, uncontrolled social experiment which poses the question, Can a society preserve any of its traditional virtues by submitting all of its institutions to the sovereignty of technology?"[32] Whether or not we consider this an overstatement, it is clear that the US's self-proclaimed "conservatives" are generally little exercised by technological transformations of the social order. Naturally, this is not because they simply underestimate the qualitative impact of new technologies, nor is it the result of an odd sort of fatalism (as though they believed that the dynamic of technological development is such that we are powerless to influence the nature and direction of its evolution). It is, rather, because the only practices whose conservation *really* interests them have to do with patriarchy and economic domination.

§

73. Louis Fischer on Lenin: "His was a fine brain squeezed into a doctrinal strait jacket [*sic*] of a priori judgments, a fine brain where dogma, once admitted, bored from within and made holes in his analyses"; John Dewey on Trotsky: "He was tragic. To see such brilliant native intelligence locked up in absolutes"; William J. Duiker, author of a biography of Ho Chi Minh, on his subject: "For many observers, the tragedy of Ho Chi Minh is that such a wondrous talent for exercising the art of leadership should have been applied to the benefit of a flawed ideology..."[33] Lucky for us that *our* rulers and political thinkers never allow any dogma to compromise their analyses, never find themselves imprisoned in absolutes, and never, ever labor for the benefit of a flawed ideology. Indeed, that such diagnoses might be applicable to many who assent to *our* status quo is simply *unthinkable*.

§

74. What is probably the single most widespread and momentous political fallacy today consists in the belief that a democratically elected ruler's exercise of violence abroad (e.g. assassinations or military attacks) is necessarily less reprehensible than a comparable exercise of violence on the part of non-elected or undemocratic rulers against people within their own country (e.g. violent acts of repression and executions). Yet, while we are correct in believing that acts of violence ordered by democratically elected rulers against *their own* citizens are less reprehensible than those which non-democratic rulers perpetrate against *their* citizens – since the former have been democratically empowered to administer violence, and so enjoy a legitimacy which the latter lack – there are no grounds for holding that democratically elected rulers' administration of violence *beyond their national borders* is necessarily more legitimate than any violence that a non-democratically elected ruler orders, whether at home or abroad. (It *may* be more legitimate, if, say, the measure bears the United Nations' authorization, or perhaps if it has an urgent, unimpeachable moral justification) In short, in assessing the legitimacy of such acts we must take into consideration both the source of the ruler's authority *and* the locale in which the acts occur. An unquestionably legitimate action, from a political or procedural perspective, is one ordered by a democratically elected ruler within his own country (that local institutional requirements must also be respected goes without saying). A democratically elected ruler who intervenes abroad is in principle acting just as *illegitimately* as an undemocratic ruler who authorizes acts of violence against his own people or in foreign lands. In both cases the ruler authorizes activities within a domain in which he cannot claim legitimate sovereignty.

The conviction, then, that the democratic rulers' actions are more legitimate because they were elected *elsewhere* rests on a crude fallacy. One reason that this fallacy proves so significant is that it obscures the democratic rulers' responsibility for war crimes and violations of human rights. Yet equally important, the currency of this fallacy makes it possible for *democracy* to serve as a cover for, and justification of, *imperialism*: since the rulers who authorize military assaults on other nations were themselves democratically elected and therefore possess exemplary democratic credentials in one domain, many conclude – fallaciously – that the enormities for which these rulers are responsible enjoy a minimal democratic legitimacy and so cannot be considered imperialist actions, which are undemocratic by definition.

§

75. The truly dismaying fact about many workers who bother to vote in elections is not that they vote for politicians and parties that, while claiming to defend labor, support and enact anti-labor policies; no, the truly dismaying fact is, rather, that they vote for politicians and parties that *do not even claim* to represent their interests. (Spanish saying: "No hay nada más tonto que un obrero de derechas" – "There's no one stupider than a right-wing worker.")

§

76. Three symptoms, or rather effects, of ideology. First, it renders one singularly maladroit in wielding Ockham's Razor: for certain classes of events, the most economical explanations are consistently eschewed or ignored; second, those who long ago forfeited any claim to credibility are still *believed*, or at the very least still enjoy the benefit of the doubt; finally, the burden of proof is systematically inverted, so that, for example, the burden of proof falls on those who claim that the imperialist countries' military assaults on other nations and support for repressive regimes is evidence of a disregard for human rights, and not on those who ascribe such policies to a principled commitment to human rights.

§

77. It is significant that with all the fretting in the United States about "dumbing down" – whether in school curricula, the media or popular culture – there is practically no discussion of what is perhaps the most momentous dumbing down of all, namely *ideological dumbing down*, a process that, having benefited enormously from the collapse of Eastern European Communism, has led to the breezy revisionism that passes for

Cold War history and the Left's craven, near total capitulation in the face of capitalist triumphalism.

§

78. E.H. Carr, the great historian of the Soviet Union, once wrote à propos of some of Trotsky's writing, "the analysis was exceedingly acute, the positive prescriptions theoretical and unrealistic."[34] Carr's observation captures perfectly the essence of much sectarian writing, and in particular much sectarian *Trotskyist* writing. It also points to the problem posed by the sectarian Left press today, that is, the question of whether or not we ought to *avoid* it. To be sure, many of the sectarians' prescriptions are hopelessly impracticable, or simply wrong-headed, and the strident language and frequent rhetorical overkill found in their papers would seem to be both counterproductive and antithetical to the kind of *rationality* in politics to which the Left is committed. At the same time, the analyses are often excellent, there is typically an attention to history that is noticeably absent from the capitalist press, and the treatment of information gleaned from the latter often provides a scathing ideology critique, as the bogus impartiality of "mainstream" media is ruthlessly, relentlessly exposed. Furthermore, if it is essential to challenge the kind of decorous understatement, the systematic "euphemization", that informs the news and analysis found in the capitalist press – a kind of sanitization that minimizes the severity and enormity, and above all the *outrageousness*, of countless everyday injustices and monstrous crimes perpetrated by states – then perhaps the stridency and polemical hyperbole of the sectarian press serve an important purpose after all. (To the extent that we accept morally neutral language to describe the everyday crimes of imperialism we involve ourselves in a kind of *moral complicity* with those who plan these crimes.) Above all, there is simply too little *objectivity* and *even-handedness*, or rather too much that goes unquestioned, too much that is taken for granted in the capitalist press (such as the credibility and honorable motives of "respectable" politicians, the permissibility of imperialist military actions or the legitimacy of the "free-market" economy), not least of all in the pages devoted to political "analysis".

§

79. It is because political participation on the part of the citizenry has largely been reduced to voting periodically that many have come to believe that *not voting* constitutes an important political statement, even in the absence of any other political activity. In reality, abstention per se (i.e. unaccompanied by any other form of political involvement) can only constitute a significant *political* act in a state where voting is mandatory and the failure to cast one's ballot punished by a fairly severe sanction; and this is why mere abstention is almost always a meaningless gesture.

§

80. *The allure of capital punishment in the United States.* It is not unusual to find Americans who profess a vigorous, principled opposition to "big government"... and think nothing of empowering their state to liquidate its own citizens.

§

81. Many liberal and left-leaning intellectuals are in the habit of condemning those members of the intelligentsia who failed to "speak out" – i.e. openly, explicitly and unambiguously declare their dissent – in the "totalitarian" countries of the former Eastern Bloc, often insinuating that such a failure to resist amounts to (or is a reliable indication of) complicity or collaboration. They engage in this sort of condemnation knowing full well that great risks attended "speaking out" in such circumstances, and that retaliation was almost certain. At the same time, these intellectuals never think of denouncing a comparable failure to "speak out" against injustice on the part of most intellectuals in "free" societies, even though the risk in those circumstances is negligible, and retaliation highly unlikely. In short, they expect nothing of intellectuals in the very societies in which one is free to "speak out" with more or less total impunity, while condemning those intellectuals who refrained from expressing dissent in circumstances in which any sort of open criticism of the government was apt to be punished.

What is most striking in the attitude of these intellectuals is not merely the fact that they expect others to take risks that they themselves would never be prepared to assume. Rather, the most striking thing is that they in effect turn ordinary canons of ethical assessment on their head. Moral responsibility – and hence *blameworthiness* – is usually assumed to be commensurate with, or proportionate to, one's freedom of action and ability to affect the course of events (considerations which would include, in the case of criticizing reprehensible governments, the information and resources at one's disposal, the risks associated with resisting state power and the possibility of actually influencing official policy). Thus, in judging most harshly precisely those whose agency was in fact most constrained, while treating most leniently those who, despite their freedom from any genuine risks and their very real opportunity to influence the course of events, fail to raise their voices, these intellectuals present us with an entirely new model for moral assessment.

§

82. "Gradualism" in politics is a luxury of the privileged, to be sure; but the acceptance of "gradualism" also often serves, certainly among the less privileged, as a token of the failure to assimilate *the finality of death*. After all, to preach the virtues of gradual, piecemeal – thus long-range – reform to the severely oppressed is in effect to ask them to sacrifice the only life that they will ever have...

§

83. Are not left-wing academics whose fields engage them politically in a direct manner (e.g. political science, sociology, history, economics, certain areas of philosophy) far more susceptible to political neutralization than those whose specialties bear only very indirectly on politics (e.g. chemistry or mathematics)? Like other professionals, academics must appear congenial to their peers, and this involves, among other things, adjusting their thinking, forms of expression, conceptual apparatus, methodology and so on to their colleagues' exigencies and expectations. Since the work of academics in

the first category is often tied to political issues of interest to them, this means that they must routinely adjust the conceptualization and expression of their political views to the canons of "respectability" or legitimacy embraced by their liberal, centrist and right-wing (as well as apolitical) colleagues. To the extent that this professional self-monitoring becomes habit, it is likely to moderate, if not neutralize altogether, many of their characteristically left-wing views – *whatever* the context, forum or occasion.

There is another dilemma for left intellectuals as a whole. It is natural for left intellectuals, qua intellectuals, to "move on" once they have studied and analyzed an important socio-political problem to their own satisfaction. As *Leftists*, however, left intellectuals behave irresponsibly, even contemptibly, whenever they "move on" to other problems before having solved *in practice*, or before having at least made some real contribution toward solving, a serious problem that they have studied and analyzed.

These questions need to be distinguished from another factor in the depoliticization of progressive academics and their repudiation of activism, namely the affinity between *academic* respectability in general, on the one hand, and *bourgeois* respectability, on the other. Given this affinity, it is no wonder that as most Leftists become "serious" academics they increasingly view political activism as, among other things, *unseemly...* just as it is no wonder that many radicals tend to feel an instinctive distrust toward Leftists who choose academic careers.

§

84. How is it that in *democracies* of all places, spirited popular participation is so often represented as something outlandish? How is that "activism" – a serious commitment to regular, active participation in public affairs and political decision-making – is so often met with incomprehension, and activists themselves treated as curiosities? The very citizens who take popular participation and social responsibility most seriously, those who best epitomize the democratic spirit, are regarded by many as... *misfits*!

§

85. If only skepticism were a *universal* "second nature", so that our masters knew that they would invariably have to *reckon with skeptics* – how many evils might be averted! No more praise for religion from the mouths of irreligious demagogues; no more paeans to the virtues of drudgery from those whose lives have been exempt from manual labor; no more of the perennial pretexts for war; no more justifications for capitalism in the name of "freedom"...

Notes

Part One

1. E.M. Cioran, *Anathemas and Admirations*, trans. Richard Howard (New York: Arcade Publishing, Inc., 1991), p. 146.

2. Friedrich Nietzsche, *The Gay Science*, trans. Walter Kaufmann (New York: Vintage Books, 1974), p. 194.

3. Friedrich Nietzsche, *Beyond Good and Evil*, trans. Walter Kaufmann (New York: Vintage Books, 1966), p. 81.

4. Francesco Guicciardini, *Maxims and Reflections*, trans. Mario Domandi (Philadelphia: University of Pennsylvania Press, 1972), p. 82.

5. Salvador Dalí, "A Beast's Repast", *Evergreen Review* 44 (1966), p. 33.

6. Norman Mailer, *Pieces and Pontifications* (Boston: Little, Brown and Company, 1982), p. 143.

7. Ludwig Wittgenstein, *Philosophical Investigations*, trans. G.E.M. Anscombe (Malden, Massachusetts and Oxford: Blackwell Publishing, 2001), p. 42.

8. Søren Kierkegaard, "Concerning the Dedication to 'The Individual'", trans. Walter Lowrie, in William V. Spanos (ed.), *A Casebook on Existentialism* (New York: Thomas Y. Crowell, 1966), p. 236.

9. Cioran, *Anathemas and Admirations*, p. 199.

10. Lisandro Otero, *Llover sobre mojado* (Madrid: Ediciones Libertarias-Prodhufi, S.A., 1999), p. 240.

11. Roland Barthes, *A Lover's Discourse: Fragments*, trans. Richard Howard (New York: Hill and Wang, 1978), p. 134.

12. Friedrich Nietzsche, *Thus Spoke Zarathustra*, in *The Portable Nietzsche*, trans. Walter Kaufmann (New York: Penguin Books, 1982), pp. 183-184.

13. A. J. Ayer, *The Meaning of Life* (New York: Charles Scribner's Sons, 1990), p. 3.; Martin Heidegger, "Letter on Humanism", trans. Frank A. Capuzzi and J. Glenn Gray, in *Basic Writings*, ed. David Farrell Krell (New York: Harper & Row, Publishers, Inc., 1977), p. 193.

14. Arthur Schopenhauer, *The World as Will and Representation*, Vol. 1, trans. E.F.J. Payne (New York: Dover Publications, 1969), p. 264.

15. Nietzsche, *The Gay Science*, p. 259.

16. Friedrich Nietzsche, *The Antichrist*, in *The Portable Nietzsche*, trans. Walter Kaufmann (New York: Penguin Books, 1982), p. 586.

17. Antonio Machado, *Juan de Mairena* II, ed. Antonio Fernández Ferrer (Madrid: Ediciones Cátedra, S.A., 1998), p. 16.

18. Epictetus, *The Handbook*, in Patrick Lee Miller and C.D.C. Reeve (eds.), *Introductory Readings in Ancient Greek and Roman Philosophy*, 3rd edition (Indianapolis and Cambridge: Hackett Publishing Co., Inc., 2006), p. 419.

19. Karl Marx and Frederick Engels, *The German Ideology*, trans. Clemens Dutt, W. Lough and C.P. Magill, in *Collected Works*, Vol. 5 (New York: International Publishers, 1976), p. 236.

20. Maurice Merleau-Ponty, *The Prose of the World*, trans. John O'Neill, ed. Claude Lefort (Evanston, Illinois: Northwestern University Press, 1973), p. 25.

21. Friedrich Nietzsche, *On the Genealogy of Morals and Ecce Homo*, trans. Walter Kaufmann (New York: Vintage Books, 1989), p. 58.

22. Seyla Benhabib, *Critique, Norm, and Utopia* (New York: Columbia University Press, 1986), p. xii.

23. *Le Mystère Pol Pot* (2001), directed by Adrian Maben.

24. René Descartes, *Discourse on Method and Meditations on First Philosophy*, trans. Donald A. Cress (Indianapolis and Cambridge: Hackett Publishing Company, 1980), p. 3.

25. E.M. Cioran, *The Temptation to Exist*, trans. Richard Howard (Chicago: Quadrangle Books, 1968), p. 152.

26. Max Weber, "Science as a Vocation", in *From Max Weber: Essays in Sociology*, ed. H.H. Gerth and C. Wright Mills (New York: Oxford University Press, 1946), p. 135.

27. Hegel, Georg W. F., *Elements of the Philosophy of Right*, trans. H. B. Nisbet, ed. Allen W. Wood (Cambridge: Cambridge University Press, 1991), p. 21.

28. E.P. Thompson, *The Making of the English Working Class* (New York: Vintage Books, 1966), p. 12.

Part Two

1. Raymond Williams, *Resources of Hope* (London and New York: Verso, 1989).

2. Noam Chomsky, *Language and Politics*, ed. C.P. Otero (Montréal and Cheektowaga, New York: Black Rose Books, 1988), p. 599; emphasis in the original.

3. John Stuart Mill, *Autobiography* (Indianapolis: The Bobbs-Merrill Company, Inc., 1957), pp. 86-87

4. Frederick Engels, *Anti-Dühring*, trans. Emile Burns, in Karl Marx and Frederick Engels, *Collected Works*, Vol. 25 (New York: International Publishers, 1987), p. 270.

5. Andrés Soria Olmedo (ed.), *Treinta entrevistas a Federico García Lorca* (Madrid: Aguilar, S.A. de Ediciones, 1989), p. 242.

6. Engels, *Anti-Dühring*, p. 268.

7. Cited in Jeffrey Brooks, *Thank You, Comrade Stalin!: Soviet Public Culture from Revolution to Cold War* (Princeton: Princeton University Press, 2000), p. 108.

8. Manuel González Prada, *El Tonel de Diógenes*, in *Obras*, Book I, Vol. 2, ed. Luis Alberto Sánchez (Lima: Ediciones Copé, 1991), p. 198.

9. Thomas Hauser, *Missing* (New York: Simon & Schuster, 1988), p. 255.

10. Herbert Marcuse, *An Essay on Liberation* (Boston: Beacon Press, 1969), p. 83.

11. J. Salwyn Schapiro, "Comment", *Journal of the History of Ideas* Vol. 10, no. 2 (April 1949), p. 304.

12. Mill, *Autobiography*, p. 149.

13. Vladimir Ilyich Lenin, *What is to Be Done?*, trans. J. Fineberg, in *Collected Works*, Vol. 5, ed. G. Hanna and V. Jerome (Moscow: Progress Publishers and London: Lawrence and Wishart,1961), p. 422; emphasis in the original.

14. Mao Tse-tung, "Problems of War and Strategy", in *Selected Works of Mao Tse-tung*, Vol. 2 (Peking: Foreign Languages Press, 1965), p. 224.

15. Carlos Franqui, *Cuba, la revolución: ¿Mito o realidad?* (Barcelona: Ediciones Península, 2006), p. 371.

16. Alma Guillermoprieto, "The Harsh Angel: The Revolutionary Who Could Find No Revolt to Please Him", *The New Yorker*, October 6, 1997, p. 106.

17. Robert A. Pastor, review of *The Memoirs of Manuel Noriega: America's Prisoner, Washington Monthly*, vol. 29, no. 6 (June 1997), p. 43.

18. Noam Chomsky, "Philosophers and Public Policy", in Virginia Held, Kai Nielsen and Charles Parsons (eds.), *Philosophy and Political Action* (New York, London and Toronto: Oxford University Press, 1972), p. 203.

19. Karl Marx and Frederick Engels, *Manifesto of the Communist Party*, trans. Samuel Moore, in *Collected Works*, Vol. 6 (New York: International Publishers, 1976), p. 504.

20. Richard Sandomir, "Tyson Apologizes for Bites, Saying He 'Snapped'", *New York Times*, 1 July 1997, p. B11.

21. Adam Smith, *The Wealth of Nations*, ed. Edwin Cannan (New York: Modern Library, 1937), p. 14.

22. Paul A. Baran, *The Longer View: Essays Toward a Critique of Political Economy*, ed. John O'Neill (New York and London: Monthly Review Press, 1969), pp. 41; 28.

23. Ralph Waldo Emerson, *Society and Solitude*, in *The Collected Works of Ralph Waldo Emerson*, Vol. 7, ed. Douglas Emory Wilson (Cambridge, Mass: Belknap Press of Harvard University Press, 2008), p. 68.

24. Clive Ponting, *Churchill* (London: Sinclair-Stevenson, 1994), p. 258.

25. Lenin, Vladimir Ilyich, *"Left-Wing" Communism – An Infantile Disorder* in *Collected Works*, Vol. 31, ed. Julius Katzer (Moscow: Progress Publishers. 1966), p. 50

26. Marx and Engels, *Manifesto*, p. 487.

27. Peter Beilharz, "Ends and Rebirths: An Interview with Daniel Bell", *Thesis Eleven* 85 (2006), p. 93.

28. Thomas Paine, *Rights of Man* (Indianapolis and Cambridge: Hackett Publishing Company, 1992), pp. 123-124

29. José Enrique Rodó, *Ariel*, in Susana Nuccetelli and Gary Seay (eds.), *Latin American Philosophy: An Introduction with Readings* (Upper Saddle River, New Jersey: Pearson Prentice Hall, 2004), p. 219; emphasis in the original.

30. Alexis de Tocqueville, *Democracy in America* Vol. 2, trans. Henry Reeve, ed. Francis Bowen (Cambridge, Massachusetts: Sever and Francis, 1863), p. 123.

31. Marx and Engels, *Manifesto*, p. 487.

32. Neil Postman, *Conscientious Objections* (New York: Alfred A. Knopf, Inc., 1988), p. 107.

33. Louis Fischer, *The Life of Lenin* (New York, Evanston, and London: Harper & Row, Publishers, 1964, p. 419; James T. Farrell, "Dewey in Mexico", in John Dewey, *Philosopher of Science and Freedom*, ed. Sidney Hook (New York: The Dial Press, 1950), p. 374; William J. Duiker, *Ho Chi Minh* (New York: Hyperion, 2000), p. 576.

34. E.H. Carr, *Socialism in One Country* Vol. 2 (London: Macmillan & Co. 1959), p. 34, cited in Jonathan Haslam, *The Vices of Integrity: E.H. Carr, 1892-1982* (London and New York: Verso, 1999), p. 187.

Acknowledgements

I am grateful to Janice Brent and Eric von der Luft for invaluable comments on preliminary drafts of this book. My greatest debt, however, is to Allan Cameron, whose sagacious criticism and advice led to countless improvements to the manuscript.

A number of aphorisms and fragments appearing in this book were first published, often with some variation, in *VOX*, no. 3; *Left Curve* 31 and 32; *Orphan Leaf Review*, no. 7; *Political Affairs*, Vol. 86, no. 1 and 2; and *Secular Nation*, Vol.12, no. 1. I wish to thank the editors of all of these journals for their assistance and encouragement.

www.vagabondvoices.co.uk

Allan Cameron, *In Praise of the Garrulous*

"A deeply reflective, extraordinarily wide-ranging meditation on the nature of language, infused in its every phrase by a passionate humanism" – Terry Eagleton

Price: £8.00   ISBN: 978-0-9560560-0-9

Alessandro Barbero, *The Anonymous Novel*

"Russians are great talkers and the novel floats on a sea of wonderfully varied, expressive and tremendous speech. ... If you have any feeling for Russia or for the art of the novel, then read this one." – *The Scotsman*

Price: £14.50   ISBN: 978-0-9560560-4-7

Ermanno Cavazzoni, *The Nocturnal Library*

"... those who enjoy the fantasies of Lewis Carroll or the grotesque lands of Jonathan Swift will find their mental landscapes widened." – *The Herald*

Price: £12.50   ISBN: 978-0-9560560-5-4

Allan Massie, *Klaus and Other Stories*

"Allan Massie is a master storyteller, with a particular gift for evoking the vanishing world of the European man of letters. His poignant novella about Klaus Mann bears comparison with his subject's best work." – Daniel Johnson, editor of *Standpoint*

Price: £10.00   ISBN: 978-0-9560560-6-1

Allan Cameron, *The Berlusconi Bonus*

"... a profound, intelligent novel that asks serious, adult questions about what it means to be alive." – *The Herald*

Price: £10.00   ISBN: 978-0-9560560-9-2

Information, text and authors' biographies on our website